HOW TO REPAIR THE INTERIOR OF YOUR HOME

Jackson Hand

THEODORE AUDEL & CO.
a division of
HOWARD W. SAMS & CO., INC.
4300 West 62nd Street
Indianapolis, Indiana 46268

ISBN: 0-672-23815-2
Manufactured in the United States of America

CONTENTS

1

FLOORS AND STAIRS

FLOORS AND STAIRS are the most vulnerable of all home construction components. They are usually unsupported from below. They must withstand the ravages of traffic and the abrasion of dirt. They are the only surfaces of the house that are frequently subjected to the effects of detergent and water. The wonder is not that you may have to work on floors now and then, but that you don't have to work on them more often.

Some of the troubles a floor can give you involve construction, and apply to both wood floors and those covered with tile or sheet materials. They are covered later in this chapter. However, the most frequent repair jobs involve work on the surfacing materials and they will be discussed first.

HOW A FLOOR IS CONSTRUCTED

Standard residential floor construction involves these elements, shown in the accompanying drawings:

• Floor framing is composed of *joists*, which are usually 2 x 6, 2 x 8, or 2 x 10 (less commonly, 2 x 12) planks on edge. First-floor joists are supported at their ends by the house foundation, or by the foundation at one end while the other end rests on a beam located halfway between two foundation walls. (If a house is quite big there may be two beams.)

Second-floor joists are supported by outside walls and by the room partitions of the first floor.

• Also part of the framing is the *bridging*, which may be in the form of an X of light lumber nailed between joists, or pieces of the same 2″ stock as the joists, cut to length and spiked in a staggered row between them. The purpose of bridging is to prevent the joists from twisting, and to distribute the load more evenly between them.

• On top of the joists is the *subflooring.* This may be composed of 1 x 6 or 1 x 8 tongue-and-groove boards or of plywood, usually ⅝″ or ¾″ thick. Subflooring of boards is most often nailed at a 45-degree angle to the joists, a further contribution to the strength and uniform resilience of the floor.

Typical floor construction in a house. In some homes, the subfloor may be ⅝″ plywood instead of 1″ boards nailed diagonally. The beam may be a steel I-beam instead of doubled-up 2 x 6s or 2 x 8s. Second-floor construction is the same, except that the joists are supported by walls rather than by foundation.

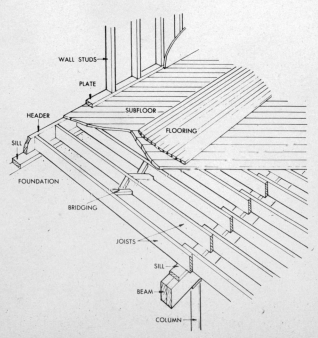

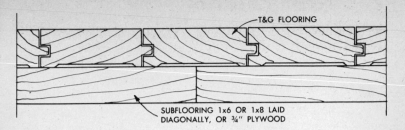

Cross-section of tongue-and-groove flooring laid on lumber or plywood subflooring.

Hardwood flooring. When a finished floor is hardwood (most often oak or maple and less commonly one of the southern hardwoods) the flooring strips are tongue-and-groove. Flooring is always laid crosswise to the joists, with the rare exceptions you may encounter in unique situations in individual houses.

Since the nails holding hardwood flooring down go through the tongue, you can never see them, except perhaps at the edges of the room, beneath the baseboard and shoemold. The strips vary in length from about 2′ to perhaps 10. Thus, any "run" of flooring is composed of two or more pieces, except in rooms that are quite small. The ends of the strips are machined true and square at the mill, so that there is rarely any gap between two lengths.

Resilient flooring. The term "resilient flooring" is often used to cover the entire range of tile, linoleum, vinyl "roll goods" and similar materials. The floor gains no strength from resilient flooring materials, and therefore the underfloor usually consists of two layers:

(1) The subfloor may be the same as for hardwood — either boards or ⅝″ or ¾″ plywood.

(2) There is also another layer called *underlayment,* carefully nailed (sometimes with adhesive) to the subfloor. The material is most often plywood or hardboard, usually ¼″ thick. Its purpose is to bridge and level off any irregularities in the subfloor, but more important, to provide a smooth surface for the resilient material. This is necessary because all

7

resilient flooring tends to "follow the floor"—that is, conform to indentations, bumps, ridges, cracks, etc., in the material it is laid over.

These flooring materials are laid in a mastic or adhesive that is troweled on the underlayment, usually with a toothed spreader that automatically measures and uniformizes the mastic.

Block flooring. One of the increasingly popular recent forms of flooring is hardwood in blocks that is laid much the same way as resilient tile. The blocks may be several side-by-side strips of regular hardwood flooring, or they may be squares of plywood faced with oak or some other hardwood. The blocks are grooved on two sides, tongued on the other two. Thus, when they are laid, the units lock together.

Although block flooring can be put down over a plywood subfloor, it is standard practice to use an underlayment over a board subfloor. The reason for this is to minimize—even eliminate—the chance that unevenness in the support of the boards would coincide with the joists in the block flooring and produce a rocky floor.

With the general character and construction of floors made clear, what are the problems you run into—and their solution?

WHEN A FLOOR SQUEAKS

A squeaky floor indicates that one or several of the structural elements covered above is letting a little slack into things. As a result, two boards rub together and produce the annoying squeak. It may be between two flooring boards; it may be between a flooring and a subflooring board; it may be between a subflooring board and a joist; it may be between a joist and the beam it rests on.

The first step is to find the squeak. You may have to listen with your ear close to the floor, or you may have to go down to the basement. Get some member of the household to activate the noise while you chase it down. To pinpoint it exactly, try laying your fingers gently across the floorboards. Quite often you can feel the vibration.

The cure depends on the nature of the construction parts involved in the squeaking.

- If the noise is caused by a friction between two framing members that are not exposed—presenting no esthetic problems—hammer some nails or spikes into the joint to stop the movement. Just in case the nails may not kill the motion altogether, squirt some oil in the crack.
- If the noise is caused by friction between flooring and subflooring and you can get at it from below, drive three or four screws up through the subflooring into the flooring. Predrill for the screws, because that flooring is hard. Select screws about a ¼″ shorter than the combined thickness of the two flooring elements, so you can be sure the points won't come through above. Draw them up tight, even using a screwdriver bit in a brace to make sure the two layers of the floor are held tight and motionless.
- You may find that the subfloor has warped upward, leaving space between it and the joist, resulting in a squeak when weight is applied above. Handle this problem by screwing a cleat (a length of 2 x 2 is good) flush with the top of the joist, just under the offending subfloor area. Then run screws up through this cleat into the subfloor, pulling it down against the top of the joist. As you make final turns on these screws, ask someone to stand on the floor above, to help make things tight.
- When flooring boards rub together, you may be able to quiet them by screwing from below—as covered in the above paragraph—provided you drive screws into both of the offending boards.
- Squeezing glue between boards that rub together and squeak will usually stop the friction. Use the kind that comes in plastic bottles with a nozzle, and force as much glue into the crack as you can, so that it will work into the tongue and groove. Keep off the floor until the glue dries.
- Lubrication is one of the simpler methods of eliminating squeaks in floorboards. Since the floor is finished with a relatively impervious material, you can actually squirt oil be-

tween the boards. Any that remains on the surface wipes away. Or you can use powdered graphite.

• A wood-swelling material (Chair-Loc is one brand name) squirted into the crack between squeaking boards swells them into such a tight fit that the squeak is eliminated — unless, of course, the crack is too wide in the first place.

In some cases, you may find it necessary to nail or screw from the top to silence a squeaky board. If you do, try to find some hardened steel flooring nails. Building supply dealers usually have them, although a hardware store may not. You can use ordinary nails — 8-penny finishing nails — if you pre-drill through the oak with a bit slightly smaller than the nails. (They'll bend if you try to hammer them through oak.) It's best to drive the nails at a slight angle, and it's even better to use them in pairs, driven at opposite angles. This gives the best grip. Countersink the nails and fill the holes with wood plastic that matches the finished wood. Spot-stain the patches to make a better match, if necessary.

When you do squeak therapy with screws, you may want to use a plug cutter to obtain little disks of the same wood as the floor, to cement into the counterbored screw holes. Again, spot stain the plugs to match.

REPAIRING DAMAGED FLOORBOARDS

It is not easy to remove and replace hardwood flooring, because the boards are tongue and groove not only at the edges, but also at the ends. Each board is locked in with its neighbors. For that reason, plus the difficulty of matching a new piece of flooring to an existing floor, it is almost always best to approach repairs with an eye toward patching, rather than replacing. Taking this approach in stages . . .

• Sanding and refinishing a damaged area is one of the easiest repair methods. The sanding, whether done by hand on a small area or by machine, should be blended into the surrounding surfaces. Be sure to avoid straight-line margins which would be more conspicuous than random curves. After you've graduated down to fine sandpaper, it may be necessary to blend and mix pale stains of the proper color to match the existing floor. Remember that the final hue will be the result of the stain, if any, plus the floor finish you use, since both contribute color or intensity to the wood.

• Filling scratches or dents in a floor is essentially the same as it would be in any wooden surface. At well-stocked paint stores you can buy wood filler of the plastic wood type in a variety of colors. One of them may be the color you want. If not, use the "natural" filler, and stain the patch when it is hard and smoothly sanded. It's a good idea to apply some of the filler to a "test" surface, so you'll have a place to experiment with stains.

• Wood patches are better than plastic wood when the scratch or gouge is large and deep. With a router or chisel and mallet, cut out the damaged area ¼″ or so deep. Then cut a piece of flooring the right size and thickness to fill the depression. If you make the patch from a piece of wood with a grain that closely resembles that of the floor, it will be inconspicuous when it is sanded and stained and finished to match.

Replacing a floorboard. Should you find it necessary to put in a new piece of flooring, it is easiest to replace an entire board, even though the damage may be confined to a small part of the strip. There is no neat and clean way to get the damaged board out. One technique is to run a portable electric saw down the middle of the board, set to cut exactly the

To insert a single board in standard floor, saw off the lower lip of the groove and the tongue of the adjacent board. This lets the board fall into place after you fit the tongue into the groove of the other board.

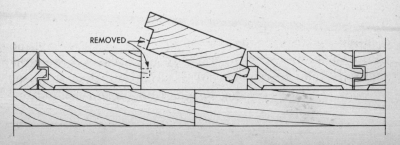

REMOVED

depth of the board. Then, you can pry the two strips out. Be careful not to damage the adjacent board. If you don't have a saw available, removing the board is just a matter of chisel and mallet.

Once the strip has been removed, use a chisel to cut the *tongue off the end* of the board at one end of the gap. Use a plane or table saw to *remove the bottom lip of the groove* off the replacement board. Cut this board the required length, *leaving the tongue end intact.* In other words, cut the scrap off the end of the new strip that has the groove in it.

To put the replacement strip in, slip the tongued end into the groove at the end of the opening. Press or pound the board into position. Since you have removed the bottom lip of the groove on the new piece, and since you have removed the tongue at the end of the cavity, the new strip will seat down on the subflooring.

You'll probably have some fairly heavy sanding to do, bringing the new piece down flush. Then custom-stain and finish the new wood.

The techniques used for handling a single board translate easily into work on several boards, with this difference:

After the first piece has been sawed or chiseled out, you will be able to use a pinchbar under the tongue edge of succeeding boards, to pry them up from the subfloor, applying the bar at the nailing points. When you have loosened the board enough, pry it up in the middle and saw it in two. Then finish ripping the two halves out.

When you put the new strips in place, start at the edge of the opening which has the flooring with the tongue. Cut the replacement pieces to length, and nail them in place through the tongues, the same as the original pieces were nailed. Sand, stain, and finish.

Replacing block flooring. The specific type of block flooring determines the specific methods of replacing damaged units. If your floor blocks are made up of actual strips of flooring, you may be able to remove a single strip and replace it, following the methods covered above. If it is made of plywood blocking, the entire square must be replaced, of course.

Owing to the tongue-and-groove design of these blocks, removal requires these steps:

1. Using a portable saw, make a cut diagonally from corner to corner, in both directions. Be sure to cut only as deep as the thickness of the block.

2. With a chisel or prybar, lift each of the triangular sections at the center of the block. They'll break loose, and let you disengage them from the tongue-and-groove joining at the edges.

3. To insert a new block, you must first rip off the tongues and the bottom lip of the grooves. This will let the square settle into the opening. Some modifications of the size may be necessary. If so, use a plane.

4. Apply adhesive or mastic and press the new square in place.

As with other wood floor repairs, it will be necessary to experiment with stain colors in order to match up the new block or strip with the rest of the room. Some block flooring is prefinished. When this is the case, you must find a block of the same finish. Color differences, then, will be those resulting from aging and weathering of the floor—perhaps not great enough to be critical. You may, however, be able to bring them closer together by brushing on a thinned coat of dark oak varnish stain, then wiping it off selectively and carefully until the remaining film provides just the right amount of coloration.

When a floor is old and badly worn and damaged, you'll find it almost as easy to put down a new floor—right on top of the old—as to make repairs. The techniques for handling block flooring and resilient floor tile are shown in accompanying photographs.

REPAIRING RESILIENT FLOORING

Damage to floor tile, linoleum, and similar materials is always

HOW TO LAY BLOCK FLOORING

Block flooring may be composed of short lengths of regular hardwood flooring, like these tiles, or it may be of plywood. In both cases the pieces are tongue-and-groove, easy to lay.

An underlayment of plywood or hardboard makes the new floor level. Nail sheets every 4" along the edges, every 8" throughout, using roofing nails.

Lay out experimental rows of blocks in both directions to determine the best spacing. Then mark a line at the edge of the row, a few feet from one wall.

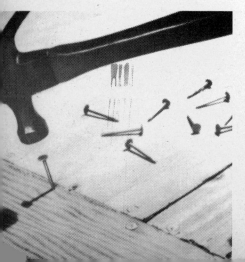

Spread the adhesive over all of the area on one side of the line, and lay the blocks in that area. This way, you have a clean place to stand.

Then, with the newly laid floor to stand on, turn around and do the other part of the floor. Be sure to follow instructions on the mastic, and be sure you snug the squares close together.

The rows at the end of the room will have to be cut to fit. The final step: nail the baseboard and the shoe mold in place. They must not be nailed tight on the flooring or they'll interfere with normal expansion and contraction. Use a matchbook cover as a spacer.

Remove a damaged floor tile by taping a sheet of aluminum foil over it, then heating the tile with a flat iron.

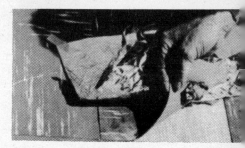

When it is hot, you can peel the tile from the floor. If any adhesive remains, scrape it up before applying new adhesive for the replacement.

repaired by replacement. That is why it's a good idea, if you have such a floor put down — or put one down yourself — to save the trimmings, ends, or extra tile. It's just about impossible to go back to the floorcoverings store a few years later and buy materials that will match.

About the only tools you need to do resilient floor repairs are a linoleum knife, a broad spatula, and a notched adhesive spreader. And, the family flatiron. To lift damaged tile, do this:

1. Spread a piece of aluminum foil over the tile, and run a hot iron over it until it softens.

2. Slip the broad spatula under the edge of the tile and lift and scrape it off.

3. Continue to apply heat to the adhesive which remains on the floor where the tile was, and scrape the area clean. Try to make it absolutely smooth, or the roughness will show through the new tile.

4. Spread mastic or adhesive with the notched spreader, and put the new tile in place.

Patching damaged linoleum or other roll goods calls for basically the same techniques, but first you must make a

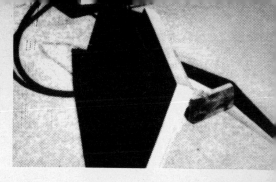

Seams often lift in linoleum installations, and water soaks the underlayment. Before you trowel in new adhesive, dry the crack thoroughly by directing a small electric heater at it, or a hair dryer. Vacuum out any debris, then glue the material back down.

patch that will be a perfect fit for the cutout area. To do this, position the patching sheet over the damage. Be careful to match up patterns, if any. Hold the material firmly in place and cut it to final size and shape with the linoleum knife. As you do this, let the tip of the knife go through the patch, and mark the exact shape of the piece on the floor.

Set the patch aside, and continue cutting the flooring material, following the line "scribed" by the knife. When you have cut through the resilient material, use the aluminum foil and hot-iron stunt to remove the old linoleum. Clean the area up, spread the adhesive, then put the patch in place.

If you discover a big difference in the color of the new piece of linoleum or the new tile, chances are the old floor has an accumulation of wax and cleaning materials. Try scrubbing the entire area thoroughly with some such strong cleaning agent as dishwashing detergent. This will take the old flooring back to its original surface, and although the match may not be perfect, it should be fairly close.

WHEN A FLOOR SAGS

There are probably very few suspended floors in the world without some degree of sag and a small amount is nothing to worry about. However, when the sag becomes severe, it indicates structural problems that may not be limited to the floor itself—and not measurable by a little unevenness under foot. The sag may signal the need for some serious bracing and reinforcing from below.

As the accompanying drawing shows, the stiffness, firmness, rigidity of a floor is provided by the heavy joists, on edge. The subfloor helps to distribute load over two or more joists, but does relatively little to make the floor strong. Further, the flooring itself contributes little to the strength of the floor.

Therefore, floor sag is always due to downward flexing of the floor joists. The reason for the bend may be excessive weight above, the inevitable "droop" over a period of time, or a warping in the lumber that occurred as it dried. This is the key to bringing the floor back to plane; the joists must be straightened, then either supported or reinforced so that they will stay straight.

When a sag in the floor develops slowly over a period of time as often happens, you may not notice it until one day is seems that a table or chair is standing at an angle. When you make that discovery, check for the exact location of the sag this way:

1. Stand furniture to one side and roll back the rug.

2. Use a board 8' or 10' long with an absolutely true edge. Check it by sighting down the length. Position the board over the suspected sag. Mark the spot on the floor where the sag is the greatest—that is, where the space between the board's edge and the floor is greatest.

3. Turn the board 90 degrees as a further check to find the low spot.

The reason you must find the precisely lowest spot is that you must apply the corrective forces to that spot, from below.

Telescoping jack-post comes in the form of two heavy tubes that fit together, held to the required length by a pin. There are flange plates for top and bottom, and a heavy threaded rod that unscrews from a socket to extend lifting pressure.

common to the room you're in and the room or basement or crawl space below. You do this as a means of locating, from beneath that same lowest spot in the floor sag.

How to use a floor jack. To raise the sag in the floor, you need a heavy-duty jack. If you're working in a crawl space, a regu- Once you have located it, determine some point of reference lar contractor's jack will do the job. You can rent one at any well-stocked rental center. If the sag is over a basement, the regular jack will be too short. Instead, use a jack-column — often called a "Tel-e-Post." This device can be adjusted to any normal floor-to-ceiling height, and is equipped with 6" or so of heavy screw drive. Here's how to set either of the jacks up for business:

1. First, you need a firm base. If you happen to be setting up on a concrete floor, this is no problem. If, however, it is a wooden floor, you must establish a "bridge" across four or five of the floor joists. To do this, lay two, three, or four lengths of 2 x 6 or 2 x 8 on top of each other, across the floor joists. Be sure they run crosswise of the joists of the floor you're standing on. This bridge will distribute the force of the jack over an area large enough to support it.

2. Next, you must provide a similar form of bridging across the sagging joists above, spanning three or four or more, depending on the degree and the spread of the sag. Usually a length of 4 x 4 works for this bridging, and it is relatively easy to handle, compared to a lamination of 2-by-stuff.

3. Position the jack between the two bridges and snug it up, to hold the upper bridging in place. Be sure it is vertical.

You are now ready to start screwing the jack upward, applying the pressure needed to raise the sag.

Important: Do not force all the sag out of the floor at one time. If you do, it may cause cracks and ruptures that will be a tough job to fix. Tighten the jack about 1/4" a day, until things are raised far enough. Although it is true that this may cause some inconvenience — if the jack has to stay in a living area for several days — it is still preferable to the damage that may arise from jacking too far too fast.

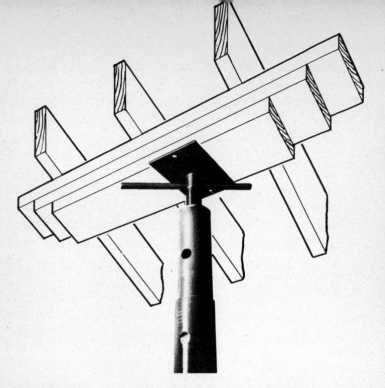

Telepost or floor jack should be capped with three or more 2 x 6s or 2 x 8s, bridging at least three floor joists. This distributes the load and reduces the chance of damage to the floor as you jack it up to remove a sag.

As the jack rises, it gradually pushes the joists back up to where they belong. It is good practice to continue the operation until the floor has been raised a bit too high — that is, until there is a slight upward bow. This anticipates the inevitability that things will settle back a little when the jack is removed. However, *if the jack can be left in position as a column* (see over) the slight over-raise is not necessary.

Making the correction permanent. In order to prevent the sag from coming back, you must either reinforce the joists while they are in the raised position, or establish some sort of support from below, to hold the joists up where they belong.

The standard procedure when the joists must be reinforced is to select some 2″ planks the same width as the joists, and spike them to the joists involved. If the sag is relatively small and the load is not great, you can usually do the job with a single plank for each joist. For greater rigidity, put a plank on both sides of the joist which runs through the middle of the sagging area.

Select these planks carefully, avoiding large knots. Be sure they are straight, although a slight edgewise bow is not undesirable since you can often spike it in place with the bow up and gain a little counter-sag force.

Force the planks up hard against the subfloor, and spike them into the existing joists with 16-penny spikes spaced the width of the plank apart—first near the top, then near the bottom, in a zigzag pattern. Cleat (bend over) the nails where they come through the joist. Then remove the jack.

If it is possible to leave a vertical support in place to hold the sag up permanently, do so. It is the best overall answer. When the jack is one you rented, you can usually replace its function with a post cut about ⅛″ longer than the distance between the floor and the bridging across the joists. This can be a 4 x 4 or a pair of 2 x 4s spiked together—or heavier timber if required. Sledgehammer it into place, then remove the jack.

You should treat this post with a wood preservative, if it rests on concrete or on any other material which might invite decay. A good way to apply the preservative is to pour it into a pail or any kind of container that is big enough and stand the post in it for half an hour or so. Let it drain.

The common practice with a Tel-e-Post is to leave it in place, where it acts as a steel column. Although you can replace it with a lally column or a wooden post, there is hardly enough saving to compensate for the bother.

Important: If you live in an old house—old enough so that it has wooden posts in the basement—it may be that sagging is caused by the gradual disintegration of one or more of those posts. You can be sure that this is the case if there is a sag in the floor near the location of a post. It is good foresight to replace all such posts with steel lally columns or post jacks.

Handling small sags and dips. There are times when a sag covers a relatively small area — hardly more than the distance between two joists. When this is the case, the problem is usually caused by a sharp warp or dip in the joist which runs across the middle of the sag. And it is usually impossible to jack up the joist to remove it.

Instead, cut a half-dozen or so wedges, quite flat in pitch, from a scrap of 2″ stock. Slip the points of the wedges in between the top edge of the joist and the subfloor, some on one side, some on the other, where the sag occurs. Tap the wedges in, starting with those nearest the middle of the sag and working alternately toward the ends. This operation will gradually lift the nails holding the subfloor to the joists, and raise the sag. If the subfloor seems reluctant to leave the joist, insert the flat end of a wrecking bar into the crack to get the separation started. Leave the wedges in place of course, after the floor has been brought up level.

SECOND-FLOOR SAG

When the sag is in a second floor, there are obvious additional problems. To begin with, the ceiling below covers up the joists. And the sag in the floor becomes, as well, a sag in the ceiling. Since the jack-and-reinforce techniques described above would require that you remove the ceiling, there are some decisions to be made.

1. Is the sag in the ceiling an eyesore — highly noticeable? If it is, correction of the sag must involve removing the ceiling material.

2. Is the sag bad enough so that the ceiling is cracked? If it is, perhaps removing it and replacing it wouldn't be a bad idea anyway.

3. Is the ceiling sag no bother — just the floor above? If this is the case, there may be a method of correcting it without jacking it up. See the next question.

4. Is the floor above a regular hardwood floor, or does it happen to be a form of tile or sheet goods that could be removed — or replaced? If it's the latter, correcting a sag may be a relatively small job.

When the ceiling must be removed. This job will be messy, if the ceiling is plastered; much less so if it is plasterboard. First you must remove the ceiling.   Be sure to spread the load of the jacking operation over several floor joists by building a "pad" of 2 x 6s or 2 x 8s under the jack.

Repairing a sag from above. When the sag in a floor over a ceiling does not call for correction of the ceiling itself you may be able to tackle the problem from above, and if you can, there are several advantages. Not the least of these is that you don't have to ruin the ceiling. And you don't have to clutter up the living space below with jacks and other paraphernalia.

The basic technique for repairing the sag from above is to take up the floor, fill in the depression with vinyl patch and other materials, as discussed below. The difficulty of the job depends on the nature of the floor. Generally, it is hard to take up wood flooring—although it can be done. And it is relatively easy to lift linoleum or tile.

Earlier in this chapter we described the basic techniques for taking up wood flooring and replacing it when it is damaged. Use these same methods raising flooring when your job is to correct a sag. If you work carefully, you may be able to save most of the strips and use them again.

To correct floor level, you must remove the flooring over the entire area that is depressed. You must first establish which way the tongues on the strips face, because you must lift the boards by prying up under the tongue edge where the nails are. Then, work "tongue-wise" across the sagging area.

When the area is bare, cut a piece of lumber with an absolutely straight edge to a length that will reach across the spot, in both directions—two pieces if the space is oblong.

Obtain some epoxy autobody repair material. Mix it according to directions, and spread it over the depressed area, using the straightedges to make sure you are bringing things back up to level. When this epoxy has hardened, check it with the straightedges. Use a chisel or heavy scraper to knock off any high spots. Mix more epoxy if necessary to fill low spots.

Work for a surface as true and level as possible.

Then replace the flooring boards you took up, adding new strips as necessary to replace any that were damaged. The final step is refinishing the floor, and it may turn out to be just as simple to do the whole thing, instead of attempting to make the worked-over area match, if it has many new boards.

If the floor is one of the resilient materials, see the steps outlined earlier in this chapter to lift it. You won't need the extra complications of epoxy patching material under a resilient floor. Instead, use the vinyl patching material sold normally for spackling at lumber or hardware outlets.

REPAIRS YOU CAN MAKE ON STAIRWAYS

Stairways are complicated, not only because they are made of many small pieces, but also because many times they are constructed to fit special situations. In addition, there are several different methods of stairbuilding — some of them done on the job, some of them in millwork factories. Some stairways are simple saw-and-nail joinery; some involve elaborate routing and rabbeting and mortising. Nearly always, the joinery is covered with moldings.

We'll begin with the basic construction:

Stairs are composed of *treads* that you walk on, *stringers* that support the treads, and *risers* that close the spaces between the treads.

In the simplest construction, the stringers are cut out in the zigzag step pattern, the treads rest on top of the horizontal surfaces, and the risers are fastened to the vertical faces. In more sophisticated stairway construction (usually done at the factory), the zigzag is mortised into the stringers, and the treads and risers are inserted in the mortises. It is common with this construction to rabbet the back edge of the tread into the riser, and rabbet the top edge of the riser into the tread above.

Squeaky stairs. Have someone activate the squeak while you pinpoint its location, both by sound and by feel. The friction that causes the noise may be at any joint in the tread-riser-stringer complement, but it is most likely to be be-

These are the main components of a typical stairway. In this model, the risers are joined to the treads with butt joints. A stairway can also be built by rabbeting the treads and the risers, as shown in the following drawing.

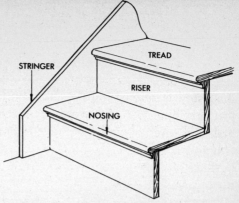

tween the tread and the riser. The simplest and surest way to get rid of it is to depress the tread as far as it will go, then drive two or three finishing nails through it into the riser. Be sure the nails go in at an angle, for maximum resistance against the tread rising. You better drill a hole through the tread, which is most surely oak and hard to drive a nail through. Sink the nail heads and fill the holes

If the riser is rabbeted into the tread, and if you don't want the patched nail holes in the tread, you can do this job another way with a lot more bother. Remove the molding beneath the lip of the tread. Predrill holes slightly smaller than the nails at an upward angle through the riser into the tread. Drive the nails. Replace the molding.

When the stairs are open below, you can take care of the squeak by gluing and screwing a strip of wood to the back of the riser, up snug against the bottom of the tread.

If the squeak occurs where the tread joins the stringers, the easiest silencing method is powdered graphite or some other lubricant. However, if the stairs are open below, you can screw-and-glue a cleat at the joint. Or, when the tread is mortised into the riser, tap in some small wedges to tighten the joint.

Replacing treads. When stairs are built in simple butt-joint manner, it is easy to replace a tread should one become worn or damaged. Simply pry the step off. Get a piece of stair tread at the lumberyard, cut it to length, and put it back. Finish it to match.

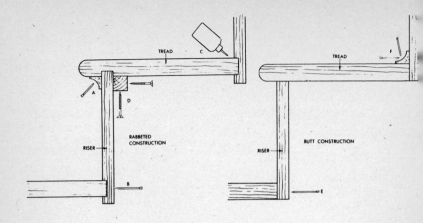

Best and easiest methods of reinforcing stairs and eliminating squeaks in rabbeted and in butt construction. A. Remove molding and drive nails diagonally through riser into stair tread. B. If steps are available from below, drive nails through riser into the back edge of treads. C. Squirt glue into the joint where tread sinks into riser. D. Screw and glue a cleat in the joint of riser and tread if available from below. E. Nail through tread into riser, angling nails for maximum holding power. F. With brads and glue, fasten a molding into the corner of tread and riser.

Things are harder when the stairway is built with mortises in the stringers, but the job can be done. Bore a hole in the middle of the tread, then use a keyhole or similar saw to cut the tread in two. Now you can pry and lift the two halves out.

Cut a piece of stair tread exactly to this length: *the distance between the stringers plus the depth of one mortise in the stringer.* Cut the rabbet in the bottom, positioned the same as the rabbet in the old tread.

By inserting one end of this new tread in the mortise in one stringer, and fitting the rabbeted joints together, you can seat the tread into position — except that the other end will not be in the mortise. So, slide the tread toward that end until it is centered, halfway into the mortise at both ends. Nail it in place, replace any moldings, and finish the new wood to match.

2

WALLS AND CEILINGS

FORTUNATELY, VERY LITTLE ever goes wrong with the internal components of walls and ceilings. The wall studs are heavy 2 x 4s, ceiling joists are even heavier 2 x 6s, 2 x 8s, or even 2 x 10s. With blocking between studs to make them even more rugged and bridging between joists for the same purpose, walls and ceilings are pretty permanent.

The story is different, however, with the surfacing materials that go on walls and ceilings. They are, in some cases, pretty delicate. It isn't hard to punch an accidental hole through a wall. Moreover, owing to the wide expanse of wall or ceiling surfaces, there are always problems with expansion and contraction and settling. The brittle, nonflexible materials used for walls develop cracks with annoying regularity. Often, you must make the same repairs several times, until the house finally settles into its permanent shape and position.

STANDARD WALL AND CEILING CONSTRUCTION

Walls are built of studs which run vertically. At the floor, there is a "sill" into which the studs are spiked. At the top of the wall there is a "plate." Spikes go through the plate into the studs.

The plate forms the support for the ceiling joists, which usually run across the narrower dimension of the room. In both cases, the framing members normally are spaced 16″ from center to center.

The wall and ceiling facing materials are fastened to the studs and joists, in one or another of these constructions:

• Wood lath, less and less common in new construction, is almost sure to be found in older houses. Lath is rough-sawn wood about 1½″ wide, about ⁵⁄₁₆″ thick, nailed across the studs or joists with deliberate spaces between the strips. When plasterers trowel on the first coat, it works into the cracks and provides an excellent link with the lath. There are usually multiple coats of plaster—a rough coat or two which builds the wall up level, then a finish coat or two of finer plaster producing the final smooth wall.

• Plaster lath is a sheet material formed of plaster between heavy sheets of paper. The construction crew nails the units of plaster lath to the wall and ceiling members, and then the plasterers go to work.

• Drywall construction is the increasingly popular use of large sheets of plasterboard, designed so that the only actual plastering required is treating the joints and the nailheads with a "joint compound."

Basic tools and materials you use for making repairs on walls and ceilings are a wide spackle knife, linoleum knife to cut plasterboard surfacing, chisel to remove loosened plaster, hammer, nails, joint cement and joint tape. Resin-coated nails are best, and they should be a size larger than those used originally on a plasterboard wall.

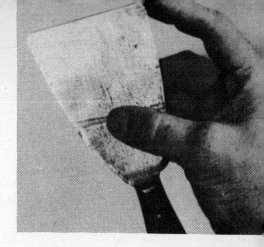

Spackle and patching knife are easiest to use if you round the corners of the blade slightly. This keeps the points from digging in, and gives you a smooth surface, easy to finish off with sandpaper.

The type of wall treatment has a bearing on the kinds of damage the wall or ceiling is most likely to suffer, and on the methods you'll find it easiest to use in their repair. For example, cracks are most likely in plastered walls which are extremely brittle and intolerant of shifting and settling. However, they are so rugged that you aren't likely to break a hole clear through them into the inside of the wall. Plasterboard, on the other hand, very rarely cracks (except at the joints). But you could ram the corner of a table into the wall and punch a hole clear through the surfacing. Another problem that often needs attention is "nail popping," caused by vibration and by wood shrinkage upon aging.

REPAIRING CRACKS IN PLASTER

It is much easier today to fill plaster cracks than it was a short time ago, and the reason is new materials for the job. Many of the old time-consuming and messy preparation steps can be bypassed entirely, because modern patching paste and powders have greater adhesion, longer working life, and different setting characteristics.

Several factors influence the choice of patching materials, and among them is cost. When a patch calls for a fairly large volume of material, something like plaster of Paris is cheap — and it works well in large volume. Smaller repairs may call for water-mix powders with special working characteristics, such as the Muralo product called "Spackle" or Durham's "Rock Hard Water Mix Putty." However, typical plaster cracks and blemishes are easiest to repair with ready-mixed spackling-patching materials of a vinyl formula, such as that produced by DAP and several other manufacturers. Adhesion, working life, and workability of the vinyl formulas make them extremely effective except when repairs are so extensive as to make cost a factor. Methods of working with each of these materials are discussed below, under the conditions where they best apply.

Most useful forms of patching materials are water-mix putty or spackle, plaster of Paris powder, and vinyl paste spackling compound. The vinyl material, ready-mixed, is easiest for most home repairmen to use, although it is most expensive. Plaster of Paris is cheapest.

Fine cracks. Some extremely fine cracks will disappear under a coat of today's thick acrylic wall paints. However, when they reach the width popularly called "hairline," run over them with vinyl patch and a putty knife. The photographs show the best method of handling the knife, which must be flexible. If you shop for one at your hardware store, test several for flexibility to be sure the one you pick will bend properly under fairly gentle pressure. When a knife bends in this manner, it squeezes the patching materials into the crack, filling it completely. It is a good idea to round the corners of

the knife slightly, with a file or stone. A blade this shape
tends to blend the patch off smoothly at the edges, while a
sharp corner may produce a groove that calls for still another
application of the patching material.

There are usually three stages in simple crack patching:

1. With firm pressure that bends the knife, force the patch
deep into the crack.

2. With minimum pressure – with the knife almost straight
– scrape the excess material off the surface.

3. With medium pressure, "trowel" the patch smooth.

As with all wall and ceiling patching jobs, you must go
over the area with sandpaper after everything is dry, to produce final smoothness. And, in some circumstances, it may be
necessary to give the patched area a texture to match the surrounding area. Techniques for this are described later in the
chapter.

It is not necessary, as is sometimes recommended, to widen
or enlarge a small crack when you work with vinyl patching
materials. And it is not necessary to dampen the crack. The
vinyl material has good adhesion and dries even in very small
quantities.

Vinyl patch in wider cracks. When there is a serious settling
or shifting of the wall or ceiling, resulting in extensive cracking in widths up to perhaps the diameter of a pencil, you can
use vinyl patch and the methods covered above. However,
you may find that the vinyl material shrinks slightly as it
hardens, making a double application necessary.

Anticipating this, make the first application with the trowel
blade well bent to force the patch deep. Then trowel off the
excess vinyl patch. With a damp cloth, wipe off all the material on the surface adjacent to the crack. This leaves you with
a smooth area to work on when you make the final application.

Preparing severe cracks for patching. When cracks in plaster
are severe – both wide and extended – there is often damage
to the adjacent material. Examine both sides of the crack for
plaster that may be loosened from the lath, or finish-coat
plaster that may be loosened from the base coat. Chip all the
loose material away, right down to *plaster that you are sure
is sound* and well bonded to the lath or the base coat.

If it is your plan to use plaster of Paris or another of the economical cementitious products for the patch, you can help make sure the new material will stay in place if you undercut the edges of the area, using an old chisel. That way, the patch fills under the lip and is "keyed" in place.

As a final step, before applying the patch, dampen the edges of the damaged area. This improves the bond of plaster of Paris and similar materials, and eliminates the chance that the patch may harden poorly because of insufficient water.

Mixing powder patching materials. There are some time-saving, money-saving tricks for mixing powder-form patching materials:

• Use a square pan, such as a cake pan or a tray from the photographic darkroom. The reason for this is the ease with which you can lift material from the tray against one of the straight sides, vs. the problems of scraping the square-end trowel up a rounded surface.

• Do not add the water to the powder. Instead, sprinkle the powder over the surface of the water in the pan. This technique serves as a sort of gauge as to the amount of powder you need, since it settles into the water. Keep sprinkling until there is no free water—and no dry powder. A little stirring then gives you a good mix.

• Estimate the volume of the damage to be patched, then use the amount of *water* it would take to fill that void. Add powder to the water, and you'll discover that you have very little material left over.

Best way to mix a powder form material is to judge the amount needed, and pour that amount of water in a square pan. Sprinkle powder over the surface uniformly, until the water has absorbed all it will take. Then stir. Straight side of the pan makes it easy to scrape up a knife-load of patch to apply to the wall.

• Read the instructions on the powder can very carefully, not only to find out tricks for using the specific patching material, but to find out what its working life may be. Some powders set hard in half an hour or less. They cannot be softened, but must be thrown out. Others, owing to special formulation, may stay in working condition for several hours. If you are working with plaster of Paris or another of the quick-setting powders, you can extend the working life by adding a little vinegar to the mixing water.

Applying the patching material. It is almost never possible to patch a large crack in a single operation. Part of the problem is the volume of patching material involved and the difficulty of troweling it smooth the first time. In addition, there is sure to be a certain amount of shrinking and fissuring, which must be caught later.

These are the steps that have proved easiest, working with a powder-mix material:

1. Glob the patch into the opening with an across-the-crack motion of the knife, working to fill the crack as completely as possible. Don't worry about a little messiness.

2. Working *with the crack,* apply pressure enough to bend the knife as you draw it along, forcing the patch in. Make repeated passes along the crack.

3. Now go over the area using the knife as a scraper, and remove the excess material.

4. Make one more pass along the crack, smoothing things as well as possible. It sometimes helps to *dip the knife in water* for this phase of the operation.

If you were lucky, the surface is now smooth. If not, let it set. Then sand off any high spots, and go at it again with patching plaster to fill any small remaining low spots. You may want to switch to the handier and easier vinyl material for this last stroke.

If the wall or ceiling you are working on is smooth-troweled, your patch will show very little if at all when it is painted. However, if there is a texture in the plaster, you must work to match it. There are several methods of doing this — all of them pretty much hit-or-miss. All must be done before the patch sets hard. Try stippling or brushing with a paintbrush or whiskbroom. Wiping with a coarse cloth or a piece of towel-

BASIC STEPS IN PATCHING ORDINARY CRACKS

1. Apply the first coating of material with strokes across the crack in both directions, to work as much patch as possible, as deep as possible, into the opening. Work fast if you are using one of the powder-mix materials with an early setting time. With vinyl and some powders, there is less hurry.

2. Force the material into the crack firmly. Best way is with a flexible knife and enough pressure to produce a bend as shown here. If there are hollows, pick up some of the furrow at side and trowel in.

3. Using the knife as a scraper, pick up the excess patching material alongside the crack. This helps avoid too much overthick area that has to be sanded down.

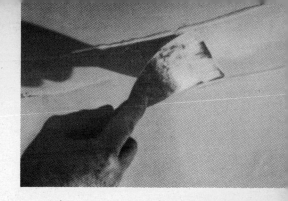

4. After the first application has hardened, come back with a touchup finish application. You can, if you wish, use economical powder materials for the first filling, then switch to easier working vinyl patch for the finish coat.

ing produces a different type of texturing, somewhat akin to the deliberate rough troweling plasterers sometimes leave. If the surface must be pebbled, you can usually make it match by painting with "sand" additives paint stores sell for mixing into wall paint. In some cases you may want to "sand paint" the entire area.

PATCHING DAMAGE IN PLASTERBOARD

Although plasterboard does not often crack the way plaster may, it may give you trouble in other ways. Sometimes the taped joints fail, and must be retaped. Nail popping is fairly common. And there is the tougher problem of a hole completely through the surface.

Nail popping. When plasterboard is installed, it is nailed along all the studs or joists. The nails are "dimpled"—that is, hit with one soft blow after they are driven home, so that there is a depression on the board. This depression is then filled with the standard joint cement. If the nails loosen, as they may when the dampish wood of new construction dries out, they push off their cement cover.

It is not enough merely to hammer them in. They will quite likely loosen again. Instead, pull one of the nails and take it to the hardware store or builder supply outlet. Get some nails the next size larger—preferably coated. Replace popped nails with these larger nails. Then trowel the dimple smooth with joint cement.

35

BASIC STEPS IN PLASTERBOARD JOINT TREATMENT

1. Glob on a thick layer of joint cement along the seam or crack. Work in distances of 6' to 8' or less, so you can move to the next step before the material starts to dry.

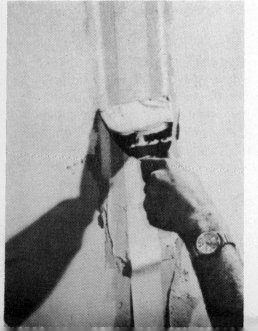

2. Apply a length of joint tape over the cement, centering it carefully and pressing it into the layer. The tape will pick up moisture and swell slightly. That accounts for the wrinkle (below wrist) as the knife forces the tape smoothly deep into the cement. You may have to lift the tape ahead of the knife, if it swells too much.

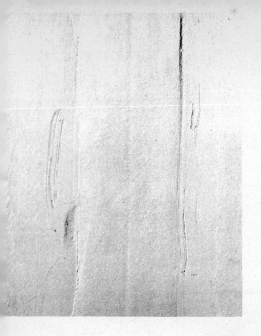

3. When the tape is imbedded, go over it with cement and make sure that it is all covered, so that no paper shows. This is important, but take pains also not to let the layer of cement get too thick, or you'll create a ridge. Depressions shown in this photo disappear with the next step.

4. Final trowel-on of cement should be thinned very slightly if it has started to thicken in your container. Skive it off on both sides (only one side is shown here) so that it comes down to zero at the edges. Finish the job with sanding when the cement is dry.

Loose tape. Plasterboard joint tape does not usually loosen unless it is soaked with water, and rarely then, unless it was improperly imbedded in joint cement when the board was put up. The first part of the repair process, of course, is to remedy the cause for the water. Then, as the accompanying photos show:

1. Rip the tape from the joint, deliberately going beyond the area of actual damage, if possible. Make sure that all the tape is removed that will come off.

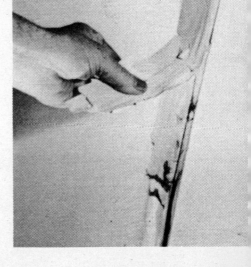

To replace plasterboard tape, tear off the loosened tape as far as it will come free, in both directions. Prod along the joint in search of bubbled tape, which indicates that more of it should be dug off. Use your knife at both sides of the crack, making sure that all of the loosened and deteriorated cement is gone.

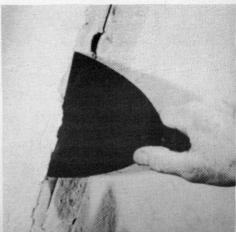

2. With a spackling knife, work along the joint, removing any joint cement that is loose or flaking.

3. Tear—don't cut—a piece of new tape the right length. Rough, torn edges are least conspicuous.

4. Run a bed of joint cement along the crack, and press the tape into this material. Then use the knife to smooth the tape and force it into good contact with the cement, all along the patch.

5. Finish the job with a layer of cement troweled over the tape, thick enough so that you cannot see the tape, but not so thick as to leave a pronounced ridge. This final cementing must extend laterally from the tape a few inches, and be skived down to zero at its edges.

If texturing is necessary, see the suggestions described previously.

PATCHING HOLES IN PLASTERBOARD

The difficulty with patching a hole in plasterboard is that there is no back-up for the patching material. The accompanying photographs show a method of overcoming this problem. Use this trick if the hole is not too large — say within the limits of about 8″ by 10″. You may want to mix up an inexpensive batch of patching powder to fill the majority of this depression, then finish it off with plasterboard joint cement or vinyl patch.

When a hole is bigger than about 8″ by 10″, use a different technique:

With a saw, enlarge the hole as far as the two adjoining studs or joists. Keep the cuts at right angles to the framing members. If it happens that there is a joint in the board at one side, break the material free. At the other side — or both if there is no joint — use a chisel to cut the plasterboard *right down the middle of the joist or stud*. This leaves you with a rectangular hole.

Now cut a piece of plasterboard to fit the hole, nail it in place, and use standard tape-and-joint-cement techniques to finish the job.

1. First cut the hole to a more or less rectangular shape, using a keyhole saw. Undercut two opposing sides, so that they bevel back under the board. Cut the other two sides so that they are beveled on the front. This trick keys the patch against movement into the wall or out.

2. Cut a piece of plasterboard about 2" bigger than the hole. Punch two nail holes through it, and loop it around a scrap of wood as shown here.

3. Insert the plasterboard through the hole, into the wall, and then snug it up tight against the back of the plasterboard by twisting the stick until the cord is tight.

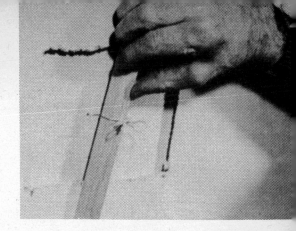

4. Fill the depression with patching plaster, working around the stick and the string. Get as much plaster in place as possible. Then, let it harden. When it is hard, cut the string away and patch the rest of the area.

5. Sand off any high spots, and finish up with a final application of patch.

WHAT TO DO ABOUT EXTENSIVE DAMAGE

If, because of something serious like a fire or extensive water damage, a large part of a wall or ceiling must be repaired, it may be simplest in the long run to cover the entire area with a new material.

For example, acoustical tile is easy to put on a ceiling, and it is no longer available only in the polka-dot pattern that once seemed somewhat inappropriate for residential use. Today's tile patterns are tasteful and beautiful—and they are effective factors in the control of sound. Installation is simple, since the lightweight tiles go up with daubs of mastic.

When large-scale damage makes a wall repair seem hopeless, you'll find it simple to apply an entirely new surface, using ⅜" plasterboard. With this thickness, it is not always necessary to replace (or fur out) door and window trim, because there is enough "reveal" to maintain a good appearance.

And, of course, there is always paneling, when it is appropriate. Modern thin plywood materials with every conceivable wood and finish as the face—or hardwood simulations—can be put up in a day or less, covering damage and adding to the appearance of a room at the same time.

MAJOR DAMAGE MAY CALL FOR
A COMPLETE NEW SURFACE

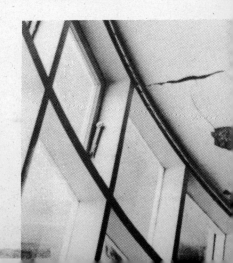

Construction shortcomings let water in over this "bow window," making patching a nightmare because of repetition. Final decision, after the bad flashing was fixed by a carpenter: Cover the area with a new surface.

Masonite is a good material for this operation, because it is rugged enough to be handled—and easily cut to fit. You could use plywood or plasterboard.

Cut out enough material on the square to cover the area. Lay it out in front of the situation, and transfer the shape to the hardboard. Mark it with chalk.

Handy saw for cutting shapes is the popular homeshop saber saw. Be sure to work with the material face down, so the roughness of the cut is on the back—that is, above, when you put the material overhead.

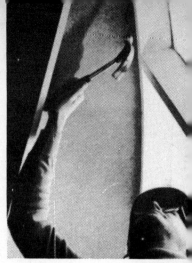

If there is final fitting to be done, use a block plane along the edge of the hardboard.

Nail the material in place with finishing nails into the joists or other framing members. Sink the nails.

Spackling compound, wood plastic, or other patching material fills nail holes and any other joints or openings, before you paint the new surface.

New ceiling of acoustical tile was the solution for extensive damage to the ceiling in this room. Installation is simple; the tiles go up with daubs of mastic.

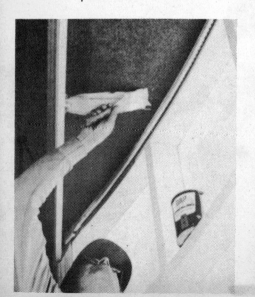

BASEMENTS AND FOUNDATIONS

Concrete is one of the world's most abundantly used construction materials, and it is often described as being "easy as mud-pie" to work with. Keep in mind, however, that there are essential guiding principles necessary to the success of concrete projects.

First, concrete and most other cementitious products *set* hard. They do not *dry* hard. In fact, it is a little recognized phenomenon that concrete will harden under water. The mix must be kept moist until the hardening and curing are well along. For standard materials, this means three or four days, although there are special formulas that set much faster, even in minutes. (See Special Cement Patching Materials below.) Regular concrete doesn't reach its ultimate hardness and strength for about four weeks. In critical situations it is important to keep the material damp for that period of time, which explains the stretches of newly poured concrete highway you so often see covered with straw or a plastic film, to retain moisture.

Once concrete or mortar has been mixed with water, *if the water evaporates before the mix hardens, it will never harden.*

Since you are working with relatively small quantities in repair and maintenance work, and since small quantities tend to dry quickly, this is an important fact to keep in mind. After the initial set, keep patches damp either by spraying them with a fine mist of water or by laying or hanging wet burlap or the equivalent over them. (When you use ready-mixed materials check the instructions carefully for any special moistening operations.)

The importance of maintaining moisture makes it virtually impossible to use ordinary concrete or mortar in any situation requiring a thin layer. When it is troweled out as thin as 1/2″ or less, the bond with existing materials is almost certain to be poor, and the chances are great that it will dry and powder without setting. (There are special materials intended specifically for thin-spread use, as discussed below.)

MIXING CONCRETE AND MORTAR
Concrete is composed of cement and a homogenous mixture of sand, pebbles, and stones or crushed rock. The latter are called "aggregate," and the material is broken down by size. "Coarse aggregate" is stones or crushed rock up to 1″ in diameter. "Fine aggregate" includes sand and pebbles that will pass through a 1/4″ screen; this is sometimes called "pea gravel."

An ideal mix has these proportions:
- Enough coarse aggregate to fill the space involved.
- Enough fine aggregate to fill the voids (spaces) around the stones in the coarse aggregate, plus about 10 per cent.
- Enough sand to fill the voids in the fine aggregate, plus about 10 per cent.
- Enough cement to fill the voids in the sand, plus about 10 per cent.
- Enough water to produce a proper working consistency, which will be a little wetter for pouring, a little dryer for trowel application.

Sand mix is a mixture of sand and cement only. It is the proper material to use when a crack or other defect to be repaired is small.

If you were involved in a project the magnitude of Boulder Dam, you'd operate on the fill-the-voids formula above, to avoid overusing the most expensive of the ingredients, cement. For your around-the-house repair work, this is the formula most often recommended:

3 parts gravel.

2 parts sand (or a bit more, depending on the nature of the coarse material).

1 part cement.

There are three elements of caution:

• All the sand-gravel-stone ingredients must be clean. 'Washed" is the word masonry material suppliers use. The reason is that any fine silt, clay, or other soil materials coating the coarses or fines — or intermixed with them — occupy space that should be filled with cement. The result is loss of strength.

• No coarse ingredient, no small stone or crushed rock fragment, may be bigger than one-half the thickness of the final job. In other words, if you were filling a depression or a crack with a minimum dimension of 1″, no element of aggregate should be bigger than ½″. In fact, many experts recommend that for cracks up to 1″ wide, *you use sand mix, with no coarse aggregate at all.*

• All elements must be thoroughly intermixed, so that the cement, sand, fines, and coarses are an absolutely homogenous mixture.

Important: Even when you buy the extremely convenient and efficient premixed cement products such as Sakrete, you should mix them at the job, to insure this homogeneity. Such bagged materials may have a tendency to jiggle into layers during transportation, with the coarses gradually migrating to the top. Therefore, when you open a bag of Sakrete, don't feel safe dipping out a shovelful and mixing it with water. It is better to empty the entire bag (on a driveway or sidewalk) and mix it thoroughly with a shovel or hoe until you are sure it is uniform. Then, use what you need and shovel the rest back into the bag. *It is not necessary to do this the next time you dip into the bag,* because the ingredients won't stratify while the bag is standing in storage.

Mixing techniques. You mix concrete as well as sand-mix on a mixing board about 4' square, in a wheelbarrow, or in a mortar box if you need only a small amount. The steps are the same in any case.

1. Thoroughly intermix the sand-pebble-gravel ingredients until they are uniform. Then spread them as smooth and level as possible, in as thin a layer as the mixing container or board will permit.

2. With a shovel or trowel (depending on quantities involved), turn the material over several times, with a lifting, sifting action. Then mix it horizontally in both directions.

Important: Cement is gray; aggregate is normally brown. Keep mixing until the color is uniform, until you can no longer see streaks of gray or brown.

3. Now form the mix into a crater or dish, heaped up in a doughnut, hollow in the middle.

4. Pour a little water in this crater. The exact amount of water cannot be predetermined, because there is no useful method of figuring out how much moisture is in the sand to begin with.

5. Scrape the mix into the water from the sides. Add more water as necessary, mixing carefully. Scrape more of the mix in; intermix it thoroughly; add more water if necessary. Repeat this until all the mixture is wet.

THE SIMPLE STEPS IN MIXING CONCRETE

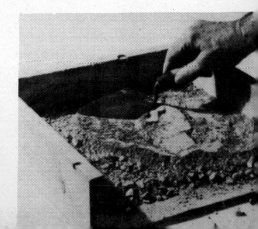

1. Whether you use a mixing board, the driveway, or a mortar box (as shown here) the first step is to spread the aggregate in a level, uniform layer. Then spread the proper amount of cement (see text) evenly over the layer of sand and gravel.

2. Intermix the aggregate and the cement thoroughly by chopping, lifting and sifting, and furrowing in both directions. Watch the color of the mix, and when it is uniform (no gray cement streaks and no brown sand streaks), it is well mixed.

3. Scoop a hollow in the middle of the mix and pour in a small amount of water. It is best to add water gradually rather than pour it in all at once, risking putting in too much.

4. Scoop the mix in from the sides of the hollow and puddle them together. Use lift-and-plop motions of the trowel, along with slicing and chopping. Bring in more dry aggregate. If you need more water, add it slowly.

5. When the mix is right, it will stand in a mound with fairly straight sides, without slumping and without draining water out at the bottom. Meanwhile, light strokes of the trowel will bring water to the top, as shown here.

Four kinds of aggregate are symbolized in this photo. For large repairs, you use "1" con mix," which includes all these ingredients. For smaller openings, the 1" stones at the left are omitted, and it becomes "½" con mix." When the crack is fairly narrow, patch it with "pea gravel mix," omitting the stones entirely. For the smallest kinds of damage, omit all the gravel and use only the sand.

How wet? There should be just a bit more than enough water to fill the voids in the mix. If you work gradually, especially as you are gaining experience with the specific batch of sand, gravel, etc., you'll notice the point where a stroke of the trowel across the top of a heap of mixture will produce a smooth, watery gleam. The gleam may disappear in a minute or two. Another trowel stroke will bring it back. This is just about right.

Keep in mind that a mix intended for use in a vertical situation, such as a wall crack, must be a bit thicker than one for a floor repair, which you can afford to mix a little wet so it will "puddle."

If you should happen to add too much water, you'll notice that it tends to pool in depressions. It is best to dry the mix by adding a small amount of dry sand only, mixing it carefully. It is usually not necessary to add any more cement unless you find that it takes a lot of sand.

Ready-mixed concrete. Mixing a batch of Sakrete or similar material does not involve the addition of cement, of course, since it is already there. But you should mix it carefully and add the water gradually, the same as with concrete you mix yourself.

Never forget that problems in masonry repair are caused by improper preparation, mixing, and application in the first place. Special care with repairs can help avoid a repeat problem.

CONCRETE IN LARGE QUANTITIES

Although the vast majority of mortar and concrete needs for repairs involves only small quantities, there may be times when you'll need the worksaving, timesaving services of a cement mixer. You can rent one in just about any community, powered either by a gasoline engine or an electric motor.

Figure your needs in cubic feet, then check with a masonry supply concern and buy a mixture of sand, pebbles, and gravel sometimes called "con mix." It comes in grades with 1″ coarse aggregate or ½″ coarse aggregate. If you're faced with the job of filling a fairly large cavity, buy the bigger stuff. Buy also, a bag of cement for every 5 cubic feet of con mix, for the standard proportion is 1 part cement to 5 parts con mix, and a bag of cement is exactly 1 cubic foot.

Mixing concrete in a cement mixer is simpler than hand-mixing, because of the thoroughness of the machine.

• While the mixer is running, shovel in five units of the sand-gravel mix. Usually the shovel itself works as a measure.

• Let the gravel work in the mixer for a minute or two, until it becomes uniform.

• Add the cement. Give this mixture long enough so that it is uniform in color—no gray streaks of cement, no brown streaks of sand and aggregate.

• Add water with a hose, gradually. When you have the right amount, the mixture will form globs on the blades inside the mixer, but the globs will slide off when the blade rotates to the top. You'll notice, too, that the rattle-bang of the stones against the mixer walls disappears and the noise becomes a swish and plop when the right amount of water has been added.

When mixing is complete, dump the load into a wheelbarrow to be transported to the job. Don't shut off the mixer without emptying it if you can help it; if you do, the mix settles to the bottom, throwing the tub off balance and often making it hard to start the rotation again.

After you dump the load—unless you'll be mixing another right away—hose out the mixer while it is running, to prevent residue from hardening and sticking to the blades or tub.

SPECIAL CEMENT-PATCHING MATERIALS

For ordinary basement floor and wall repairs requiring a cement mixture, it is cheapest to use standard ready-mixed or mix-it-yourself materials covered above. This is particularly true when large quantities are involved, on account of cost.

There are, however, certain jobs, and certain crisis situations, which call for special materials. And today's market is full of formulas containing chemicals that give you performance far different from that you get from ordinary cement mixtures of concrete or mortar. Here are some of the most useful.

Hydraulic cement. This material is a modification of ordinary cement-based mix, but it hardens in just a few minutes. It is the right material to use when a foundation or floor is actively leaking running water. (See below.) You may want to use it for many small repairs, because of its convenience. But it is expensive. A can the size of a 1-pound coffee can costs $2 or more.

Specific instructions for mixing and use are printed on the container of any hydraulic cement you buy, but some generalizations may be of value. First, the stuff sets so rapidly that you must not mix more than you'll use in about three minutes. Second, it is not normally recommended for cracks less than 3/4" in width or depth. Third, it is intended for use more like putty than cement: It must be pressed into place with a minimum of troweling or rubbing.

Air-drying cement. This material defies the law that says you must keep a patch wet. It is not truly a cementitious product. Unlike regular cementitious products, it will not set under water. This product handles like sandmix, and dries hard in a few hours. (An example is Patcho, made by Roxseal, Long Island City, N. Y.)

Expanding cement. The usefulness of this material comes from the phenomenon of expansion during curing. Once it has been applied, and after the initial set, the cement expands. It forms a tight plug in cracks or holes, although it is not intended for use in an active-leak situation. Most major cement manufacturers produce "expansive cement."

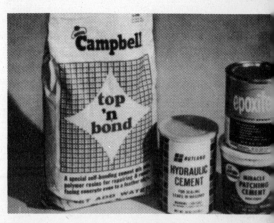

Special patching materials include Top 'n Bond, intended for surface smoothing right down to a thin edge, hydraulic and patching cements that harden in minutes and are essential for active leaks, and plastic materials such as Epoxite, which is not a cementitious product at all. Rather (*below*) it is a bag of plastic jelly and a bottle of hardener, intended for sealing very fine holes.

Surface coating. Some cement products are intended specifically for use in thin layers, or as a topping material. Examples are "Top 'n Bond," part of the Sakrete line, and "Thorocrete." The mix can be used about as thin as you can trowel it, and special polymers in the formula produce a bond in situations where ordinary cement would dry and turn to powder. It can be used, also, for ordinary patching where a sand mix would be appropriate.

Paint-on sealer. Products like Thoroseal mix with water to a thick paint consistency and go on with a brush. They seal walls that may be transmitting moisture through the concrete. They go over concrete block, almost entirely eliminating the block-and-mortar pattern. You can also use them for small patches when regular patching materials aren't available.

Epoxy sealers. Not actually a cement product but very useful in wall and floor patching are epoxy materials such as Boyle-

Trowel types you find handy in masonry repairs: 1. Mason's trowels in two sizes, the smaller usually most workable in repair work. 2. Tuck-pointing trowel, used to apply mortar to cracks or joints between blocks or bricks. 3. Short and wide plastering trowel used for applying concrete or plaster. 4. Longer, slimmer plastering trowel used for smoothing.

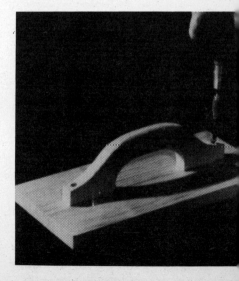

Wooden float produces a sand-textured surface, as opposed to the perfect smoothing of a steel trowel. Make a float as simply as this, with a scrap of 1 x 6, a cutout and rounded handle, and two screws.

Handy tools for cleaning up cracks before you add new material are: 1. Mason's hammer with a chisel-like end used for chipping and in masonry replacement, for breaking brick or block. 2. Coarse, heavy carborundum stone for grinding away unwanted cement or mortar. 3. An ordinary cold chisel and two special chipping chisels, for working loose material out of cracks, and for shaping a crack for proper repair.

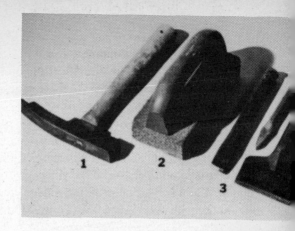

This is a hawk, used for holding a batch of repair material up against a vertical surface so that you can scrape it off and into a crack. Make it from a piece of plywood about a foot square, with a 5" length of closet pole or equivalent for a handle, fastened on with a screw. Hawk shown has an aluminum top, easier to use, easier to clean.

Midway's "Epoxite." You buy a bag of jelly-thick plastic and a bottle of activator, mix them in the can, and brush them over areas that leak, *but not while they are leaking.* The material must go on dry surfaces. Generally speaking, the epoxy materials (at something like $6 a quart) are not intended for *filling*, but rather for *sealing*. It is recommended that you fill cracks and openings with hydraulic or with ordinary cement, then use epoxy as a sealing topcoat.

BASIC BASEMENT AND FOUNDATION REPAIRS

Repairs of damage or deterioration in basements and foundations fall into two classifications: the dirty, difficult, messy jobs that involve leaks, and the mud-pie jobs that involve only dry cracks, mortar failure, etc.

These are again divided by two questions: Can the repair be done from the inside, or must it be done from the outside? Is the repair above the surface of the ground, or should the earth outside the wall be, properly, dug away?

When the latter situation exists, you may be wise to turn the whole business over to a professional, because there can be a lot of labor involved.

Cracks and other voids are easy to fill, and small leaks are easy to plug, as discussed below. However, there are considerations beyond mere repair.

• If a crack opens again after you patch it, and it seems to be a continuing repair job, you can be sure that there are structural shortcomings which should be attended to. Study the area to see if you can determine the reason for and the seriousness of the problem. For instance, if a wall bulges or seems to skid at the base or at a corner, or if a crack reappears at the top of the wall, you can be sure that there are undue pressures from the earth outside. You need a contractor to take care of the problem.

• If a wall leaks pretty generally, not merely in one place, the call may again be for the contractor, because the man who put in the foundation probably did an inadequate job of waterproofing the outside surface of the wall. To take care of the situation, somebody may have to dig away the dirt, clean the wall, apply asphaltic waterproofing (or plastic) and shovel the dirt back in place. Carefully—to avoid cutting the protective film.

• If a basement tends to leak all along the base of the wall, it's a good sign that there is a "head of water" producing excessive hydrostatic pressure, and it may be necessary to dig down and install drain tiles along the footing, which should have been done in the first place. This lets the water drain off without building up such great pressure at the base of the wall.

However, an attempt should be made to make the required repairs in a simple way first, without inviting in the expense of an outside contractor.

THE RIGHT WAY TO FILL A CRACK

While working with concrete is simple, there are some critical steps involved in simple crack patching, some of which are not often adequately emphasized.

Fine cracks. When cracks are 1/4" wide or less, it is difficult to handle them with regular cement mortar, because of the drying problem and the difficulty of working the patching material deep enough to fill the space completely. It is sometimes advisable to chip and chisel these cracks until they are wider. *It is much simpler to use a special material intended for small cracks.* Special-formula fine sand mixes, such as Patcho and E.Z. Perma Cement, can usually be worked into small cracks without the need for chipping. (Be sure to check the label to find out whether the material must be kept wet for how long.)

The technique of using these materials, normally covered in excellent detail on the labels, involves simply knifing and troweling the mix deep into the crack. If you jiggle the tip of the trowel along the crack after it is nearly filled, you can be fairly sure that the fines of the mix have worked to the depth of the crack. When you've worked in all the patching material the crack will take, trowel the surface smooth. After the initial set, you can use a whiskbroom or other tool to simulate the texture of surrounding material.

Patching wider cracks. Although the special-formula materials work in larger spaces, you can save money by using ordinary sand mix or pea-gravel mix that you stir up yourself or buy already mixed. These are the steps:

1. If necessary, widen the crack to at least 1". Avoid

"dished" or beveled edges that would result in a thin-edge patch, subject to drying before setting. It is sometimes recommended that you undercut the edges of a crack, to form an inverted V. Although this "keys" the patch into the existing material, its major function is to avoid a thin spread of concrete or mortar. Actually, a square-cut edge will do this. When it is difficult to chip a crack to the desired shape, you can avoid trouble by filling it with ordinary materials to within 1/4" or so of level. Then, finish off with a material such as Patcho, Top 'n Bond, or Thorocrete, which will harden even at a feathered edge.

2. Be sure that all loose or crumbling material has been chipped loose. Clean out dust, particles, flakes with a broom.

3. Saturate the crack with water—thoroughly. Let it absorb all it will. Mop up the excess.

4. Mix a cream-thick batch of pure cement and water, "neat cement" and water, as it is sometimes called. Swab or brush this mixture on the presoaked crack. *This is an important step, very often overlooked.* Its purpose is to condition the crack ideally to accept the patch with a perfect bond.

5. Lay in the patching material, taking pains to work it into the depth of the crack. Be sure there is a little too much so that you can puddle it in place.

HOW TO PATCH A CRACK
IN A CONCRETE FLOOR

1. With chipping chisel and hammer, knock loose all fragments of concrete at the edges of the crack. At the same time, widen it to a minimum of 3/4". 1" is better. Cut the edges square, or undercut them. In no circumstances leave a V edge.

2. Brush and flush the broken chips and fragments from the crack. If possible, use a garden hose to make sure the crack is clean.

3. Dampen the inside surfaces of the crack, if they have not already been dampened in the flushing.

4. Prepare a surry of cement and water about the thickness of paint. Brush this "bond coat" on the surfaces of the crack. Its purpose is to provide a better bond than you'd get applying the patching material directly to the dampened concrete. Since the patch must be placed while the bond coat is still wet, have the material ready.

5. Fill the cavity with the mixed concrete and puddle it with the trowel, to make sure that it works into all the spaces. There should be a slight mounding of the material, as insurance that the crack is full with no voids.

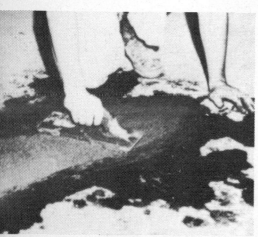

6. When you have worked the mix well into the space, use the trowel as a "screed" and scrape off the excess.

7. Use the trowel (or a wooden float for a "sand" finish) or smooth the patch and make it match the surrounding surface. Keep the patch damp for three days, unless the material is one of those with special ingredients (see text). *Photos courtesy of Master Builders.*

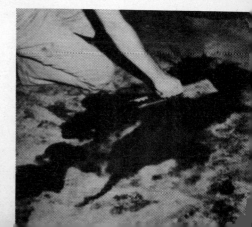

6. Screed off the excess with a steel trowel or wooden float. The float will give a sand-textured finish.

7. If you want a smoother finish, dress the patch with a steel trowel. Or produce the texture you want with a whisk-broom or other tool.

Important: It is absolutely necessary to keep the patch wet for at least three days, unless it happens to be one of the special materials. Read the label. As soon as the patch has set hard enough so that it will not wash away under a fine spray, dampen the entire area. Do this two or three times a day, unless you devise some means of cloaking the patch with wet burlap or the equivalent.

Cracks on vertical surfaces. The processes involved when you patch a vertical crack are the same as for cracks on the horizontal, but there are some differences in technique.

Unless the quantities are so large that economy is a factor, use hydraulic cement or one of the other quick-setting materials. This reduces the chances that your mix will sag out of the crack while you are applying it or before it sets.

1. Start at the bottom of a crack that runs vertically or on a steep slant. Work the patching material in, progressing upward, so that each addition is supported by the concrete below it.

2. Work with as thick a mix as possible, that is, with as little water as possible. This will help prevent sagging.

3. Although you must wet down the area and you must use the application of neat cement and water, let the surfaces dry a little more on vertical patches than you would on horizontal work. This also helps keep the material in place until it bonds and sets.

In extremely difficult situations, you may find it necessary to position a board or a piece of plywood over the crack, holding it in place with braces slanting up from the floor or even reaching across the room. This board should cover, as snugly as possible, the entire crack except for an opening at the top. Through this opening, ladle the patching cement in small trowelfuls, tapping on the board to encourage the material to

HOW TO PATCH VERTICAL CRACKS
IN CONCRETE BLOCK

1. As with any crack, chip away loose material. Work beyond the apparent limits of the crack, to be sure you remove defective masonry that might come loose later.

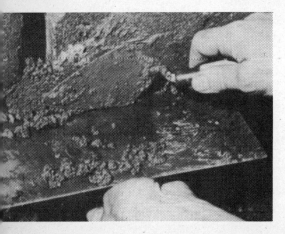

2. Mix the repair mortar as heavy as possible, that is, with a minimum but adequate amount of moisture. Use a trowel or hawk to support the mixture against the wall while you shove it into the crack. *Important:* Start at the bottom and work up.

3. After the heavy mixture has set slightly, use a thinner mix (with a little water added) to trowel the patch smooth. Keep it wet for three days, unless you are using a quick-setting material that doesn't require prolonged wetting.

settle to the bottom. When the patch thus applied has set, you can smooth it with one of the materials intended for thin-layer use.

Don't forget to keep the patch damp for three days or more, to be sure the concrete sets properly.

HOW TO REPAIR MORTAR JOINTS IN BRICK

1. Clean out loose or cracked mortar with cold chisel or screwdriver.

2. Remove all loose mortar by flushing with hose or with stiff brush and water.

3. While joint is still damp, fill with mortar. Use a tuck-pointing trowel to press the mortar firmly in place.

4. Scrape off excess mortar and finish joint to match rest of wall. After about five minutes, brush across joint to remove excess mortar on sur-rounding brick and finish again.

Patching water leaks. If you have a leak in basement wall or floor that dries up periodically, giving you a chance to work on it between floodings, the same techniques apply as are covered above. It's best to use hydraulic cement or an expansive cement, because of their extra sealing value.

When a leak is present all the time and must be patched wet, pick a hydraulic cement and follow these steps:

1. Chip away existing material until the crack is at least 1" wide and deep. This is critical, because a certain amount of volume is necessary for the patching material to do its job. Be sure to cut square or undercut; do not cut a V-groove.

2. Use a garden hose and water pressure to flush away loosened masonry and dirt.

3. Mix the hydraulic cement with just enough water to produce a consistency similar to that of glazing compound or putty. Mix a small amount, since it must be in place within three minutes of the time the water is added. Experience will tell you—with each repair job—how much hydraulic cement you can mix and apply in three minutes.

4. You do not "grout" hydraulic cement, that is, you don't count on it flowing into the crack. It must, instead, be pressed in, either with your palms or a float. Do not use a troweling action. Just press it in, glob by glob. Prolonged contact with the material will dry your skin; use gloves, or be quick to rinse your hands after use.

5. Keep hydraulic cement patches wet for at least 15 minutes. (Read the label; the wet period may vary from product to product.)

ACTIVELY FLOWING LEAKS

You can patch a leak in a basement wall or floor that is actually pouring a stream of water, using hydraulic cement. The trick is to study the crack in search of *the point at which the pressure is greatest.* After opening and undercutting the crack, start at the ends, and gradually work the cement in, glob by glob, until the only remaining unfilled space is that where the water runs most vigorously, where the greatest pressure is. Work to make this final opening as small as pos-

When a leak in a basement wall is pouring water, use hydraulic cement to plug the hole. After mixing the cement, hold it in the hand for a minute or two until it's dry, then shape it to match the shape of the hole. Press it firmly in place and hold it until it has set. Shave off excess with trowel before the cement hardens.

sible, consistent with the pressure and the amount of water. Finally, mix a batch of hydraulic cement large enough to plug the remaining hole. *Do not apply it immediately, however.* If you'll hold this mix in your hands for a minute or two, you'll feel it turning slightly warm and it will give the appearance of drying a little. Shape the glob to match the shape and size of the final hole. Press it firmly in place and hold it there for a few minutes, until it has set. Then, if necessary, use the edge of the trowel to shave the excess material off, before it finally hardens.

WHEN A WHOLE BASEMENT WALL LEAKS

Sometimes a leaky basement wall doesn't confine itself to specific cracks, but seems to leak all across its surface. This condition makes itself evident in dampness—a beading of water droplets—over all or most of the wall. This condition, however, may indicate condensation of moisture from over-humid air in the basement instead of a water-permeable wall. If cold water pipes in the basement tend to drip, if there is a damp feeling to metal surfaces, be suspicious of condensation. One way to check it out is to stand a piece of glass tight against the wall in contact with the concrete, and leave it there overnight. In the morning, if the glass is dry but the wall back of it is wet, you know that it is not condensation.

Treatment of a "bleeding" wall is almost the simplest of all wet basement techniques. It hinges on a cementitious paint product such as "Thoroseal" that mixes with water and goes on with a brush. The slurry you paint on is white and the wall is not only dry, but it is a gleaming white. Homeowners often use Thoroseal to treat a wall that doesn't leak, just to get rid of the banality of a concrete block or concrete basement wall, and to brighten the area.

The slurry flows into the pores of the concrete, poured or block, and seals them against transmission of moisture.

Important: A cementitious product such as Thoroseal cannot bond to paints or other coatings. Therefore, if you have a leaking wall that has been painted, it may be necessary to sandblast the entire surface. This is most often a job for professionals. If the area is small, you may be able to clean it up with a water-wash paint remover (such as TM-4), taking special pains to scrub the surface clean with a stiff-bristle broom as you rinse off the remover. Even so, sandblasting is a more certain procedure.

PAINT ON WATERPROOFING MIX TO SEAL A WALL

1. Special cement formulas such as Thoroseal can be used for small mortaring jobs as well as brush-on coating. Here, a cove is troweled along the base of a wall, as the first step in waterproofing and decorating a wall that tends to "weep."

2. Critical step in applying brush-on coating is prewetting the wall. Good way to do this is to spray a few feet ahead of yourself as you work along the wall. Fine spray dampens without excessive runoff.

3. Big fiber-bristle brush is the right tool for applying cement paint (although a pushbroom does a fast job if the area is big). Apply the material first as though you were troweling it into the depressions. This insures a good fill.

4. Then, with less pressure on the brush, "tip off" the application, leaving it smooth as shown here. Tipping off must follow rather quickly after the initial application, before material starts to set.

Leaks at the base of a wall. Standard construction procedures invite a weak point where a foundation wall rests on a basement floor. The builders lay the slab for the basement floor. Then they lay up block or set forms and pour the basement walls. If the concrete floor is "green" and clean, the bond between the floor and wall may be a perfect joint. Given a little time lag or a little dirt, it may not be.

That is one reason why many basement leaks are at the juncture of wall and floor. The other reason is that the hydrostatic pressure is greater at that level than at any point above.

To reinforce and repair the joint between wall and floor, be sure to pick a strongly adherent material, one that utilizes sand only, rarely any coarse aggregate. Combine these critical materials with all of the concrete-mix precautions of this chapter.

To be doubly sure of adhesion, you can buy additives for concrete (such as "Acryl 60" made by Standard Dry Wall) that you mix with water. Such extra adhesion is important when you are working a base-of-the-wall leak and don't want to chip excessively to provide a physical bond for the batch.

Leaky basement addenda: A basement doesn't leak if the entire job of design, engineering, and construction of a house was well done. However, there may be inadequate drain-away of the spill from rain-carrying systems. There may be improper pitch toward basement and foundation walls, so that water flows to the house, down the foundation, and forms pressure at construction joints which they may not be able to withstand. It may be that a house was built on a piece of land with a water table so high that the basement or crawlspace is sitting in a sea of water at least during the wettest part of the year. Although there is nothing you can do about the water table, a landscape contractor can usually modify the pitch of the land in a way that lets surface water drain away.

SMOOTHING ROUGH CONCRETE SURFACES

When a basement floor or wall is rough, due to scaling or other imperfections, the only feasible method of making it smooth is with one of the cement materials especially formulated for extremely thin application. For example, "Thorocrete," the acrylic-modified cement made by Standard Dry Wall, can be spread only ⅛" thick or less and still perform properly. Top 'n Bond does the same job.

Floors. Go over the surface carefully with a stiff broom and if you note any scaling concrete, clean it down to sound material with a hammer and chipping chisel. If there are oils, paints, or other dirt on the floor, use a strong detergent to remove them. Hose the surface thoroughly with plenty of water. Keep it damp as you apply the surfacing material, but without puddles of water.

Follow these steps:

1. Mix a thin slurry of the surfacing material, and apply it with a heavy bristle brush or a push broom, as a bond coat.

2. Mix the trowel coat fairly thick, in quantities you can apply in about half an hour.

3. Apply in a layer just thick enough to level the floor, while the brushed-on coat is still wet.

4. Use enough trowel pressure to force the surfacing into all depressions, but do not overtrowel. Typical surfacing materials tend to foul the trowel. Keep it clean by rubbing it frequently over a wet cloth.

Specific instruction sheets for thin-use materials vary. Read them carefully, since some of the methods recommended may run contrary to standard concrete procedures.

Walls. Smoothing a rough concrete or concrete block wall is easy to do with brushing-consistency mixtures of Throseal, Top 'n Bond and similar products, applied this way:

1. The wall must be free of paint, oil, and other materials that interfere with bond. Chip away any loose or loosening bits of masonry.

2. If there are fairly large depressions or cracks, fill and trowel them smooth and level. Give these fills time to set, depending on the material used.

3. Mix the brush-on surfacing materials in a quantity you can apply in no more than thirty minutes.

4. Hose the wall down with clean water. Let the water drain until the surface is damp, not wet.

5. Use a big fiber bristle brush and apply the coating in a swabbing motion that lays on a smooth coating. (See photos.) The action of the bristles both spreads the material and "trowels" it into depressions. The brush marks will show, as there is no "leveling" that you'd expect from paint, so take pains to produce an attractive texture. The best appearance usually comes from an every-which-way brushing.

The application of Thoroseal and similar surfacing materials waterproofs a wall. If water presents a serious "weeping" problem, many experts apply a coat to the lower half of the wall, where seepage pressure is greatest. Then they coat the entire wall, thus double-coating the surfaces that may need it most.

TILE AND COUNTERTOPS
IN BATH AND KITCHEN

THE TILE USED IN bathrooms and often kitchens, and the
plastic countertopping used in both kitchen and bath are
among the most troublefree and durable of all household
construction materials. The major problems come from failing
adhesion with either tile or the "decorative laminate" used on
counters and, now and then, walls. However, a tile is broken
occasionally—someone may put an over-hot pan on the
counter top—and the damage calls for patching.

THE MECHANICS OF WALL TILE

You find more ceramic tile than any other kind, although
there is a lot of plastic tile and some enameled metal tile
around. The latter are nearly always held in place with a
mastic; ceramic tile may be in mastic or actually bedded in
plaster. For ceramic tile there is a material called "grout"
that fills the spaces between the tiles. Plastic and metal tile,
being thinner, makes use of the mastic as a grout. Either way,
the purpose of the grout is to seal the wall and make it watertight.

Although it takes experience and practice, few handymen
have to handle tile set in plaster. The convenient, attractive

and long-lasting squares are easy to install, repair, and maintain—with three improvements on the old techniques:

• The use of a smooth, water resistant material such as
asbestos board for a back-up.

• The use of easy-to-spread, waterproof mastics for adhesion.

• The use of plastic-based materials (instead of cement
products) for grouting.

THE KINDS OF TILE YOU FIND IN A HOUSE

Three kinds of tile are ordinarily used around the house.

Glazed tile is the shiny stuff, usually white on the back,
with the color and glaze only on the exposed area. This is the
kind of tile you find on walls, in shower stalls, on back
splashes, and sometimes on counters—anyplace where wear
and abrasion are relatively small. Cleaning is wipe-up easy.

Quarry tile is the same clear through. The surface is not
glazed. Instead, it is matte, tough, capable of accepting con-
siderable rough traffic. It is used on floors, although sometimes you find it used on heavy-duty counters. (The name
doesn't come from "stone quarry," but is rather a corruption
of the French word for square.)

Pavers are heavier, often bigger tiles used on decks or
patios, stoops, walks, and other extra-heavy wear areas.
Because of their size and thickness, they are still most often
laid in a concrete base, unlike the glazed and quarry tiles.

You find all of these tiles in a variety of sizes and shapes,
including hexagonals. Sometimes the smallest tiles are called
"mosaics." In the rectangular groups are matching sizes
composed of a single square, two-square shape, and a four-
square shape. These shapes work together in ashlar patterns,
either in a single color or in several matching or comple-
mentary shades.

While standard wall tile, measuring 4¼″ x 4¼″, and the
larger pavers, are normally handled as individual pieces, some
of the smaller sizes are unitized into sheets, so that a fairly
large area can be covered at one time. The methods of unitiz-

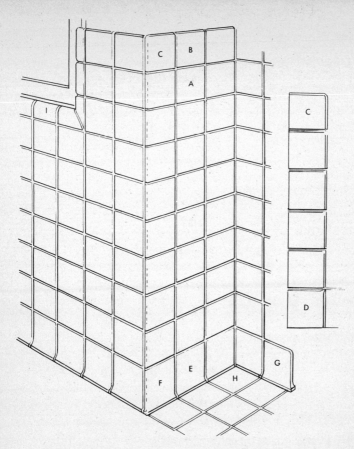

Ceramic tile for walls and floors comes in a variety of pieces:
(A) full tile; **(B)** surface cap; **(C)** outside corner, down; **(D)** inside
corner, up; **(E)** cove base; **(F)** left-hand cove corner or end; **(G)**
right-hand cove corner or end; **(H)** floor tile; **(I)** bullnose tile.

ing vary, but one common method is a group of small tiles
fastened to a sheet of heavy paper with a water-solvent glue.
Since the tiles are fastened to the paper, face side down, and
they are laid paper side up, all you have to do is soak off the
paper after the unit is laid and its adhesive has set. In another
form, a mesh on the back of the tiles holds them in unit form,
and the mesh simply disappears into the mastic when you lay
the tiles.

In addition to the tile forms you find around the house, there are coves for use at the floor, nosings for use at the top or edges of a tiled area, at inside and outside corners, and even three-plane corner for use where two walls and the floor meet. You may find that these special forms match the color of the tile, but quite often they are black, as a compromise which goes with all colors.

When replacement of tile is necessary, you can ordinarily find the shape and the color you want at a well-stocked tile outlet.

THE FOUR STEPS IN A TILING JOB

Whether you are doing repairs or installing tile over a wall area as a means of making it presentable, four steps are involved: a good sound base, proper adhesive, laying the tile, and a careful grouting job to fill and waterproof the cracks.

A base for tile. Since tile has little or no flexibility in its joints, the surface you put it on must be fairly rigid. On a floor, it must be *quite* rigid. Normally any standard wall is sound enough structurally. On an existing floor, there should be an underlay of plywood. The thicker the plywood is, up to ¾″, the better the subfloor. Use good-one-side plywood, not sheathing grade, because the irregularities in sheathing plywood may cause unevenness in the tile. In a bath or any other watery environment, the plywood should be exterior grade — waterproof.

If you discover much damage, a great deal of cracking in the grout between tiles, many loose tiles, it may be that the original underlay was inadequate. When this is true, repairs must include *new underlay* on top of the old, or the damage will surely come back. This means, of course, lifting the old tile with a stiff trowel or garden spade and replacing it with new, unless you are up to the tedious job of cleaning the old tile for reuse.

If the existing subfloor is of plywood, but perhaps too thin, you can usually make it firm and smooth enough with ⅜″ or ½″ plywood, nailed every 8″ in both directions and every 4″

along the edges. The addition of this much thickness to the subfloor will not ordinarily produce problems with bath fixtures, and you will find it possible to grout neatly where the floor meets the wall, even if there is a cove base in the room.

When the floor is a bath or laundry, etc., it should have a waterproofing-priming coat, a material you'll be able to buy at the same outlet where you buy the tile. These primers vary enough to make it important to read instructions carefully, to be sure you end up with a base which will not, in the future, soften and swell and give you repair troubles.

In severe moisture situations, such as a shower stall, the plywood base is augmented with a troweling of concrete at least 1″ thick, or with a sheet of ¼″ asbestos board layed in a waterproof mastic. Provision must be made, of course, for the drain in either case. (Plumbing supply houses sell a "shower pan" of lead or copper, complete with drain hole and hardware, which requires only a cement-and-sand lining, then tile.)

Shower walls are at their best with a substrate of asbestos board, cemented in place. Not only is it an excellent surface for mastic-tile compatibility, not only is it resistant to water damage, but it also has excellent dimensional stability, shrinking and swelling only slightly with changes in moisture and temperature.

Ordinarily, counters in the kitchen or bath need only a firm plywood base, properly primed, for an excellent tile job.

Tile adhesives. Most paint and hardware stores and the mail order catalogs all provide mastics for tile setting. There are various kinds, ranging up to epoxies for maximum adhesion and resistance to moisture and chemicals. When you buy the adhesive, tell the tile dealer what sort of a base you are planning to put it on. He will recommend the required adhesive.

It's best to buy a toothed (or notched) spreader, although you can make one by filing teeth in a piece of ⅛″ hardboard. It is important for the teeth to be spaced according to specifications, for the mastic and to be the proper depth. On most

TRICKS THAT HELP MAKE LAYING TILE EASY TO DO

1. Start tiling a plain wall by laying a row across the floor, using a glob of mastic on the back of each tile. For proper spacing side to side on the wall, see the text.

2. Use a level to make sure that bottom row is absolutely horizontal. The space at the floor may not be exactly true — but that is better than having the courses up at eye level look crooked. Chips of tile, scraps of wood, etc., can be used to true the course.

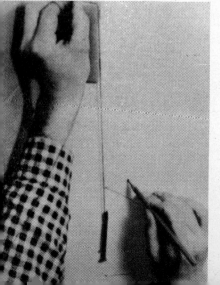

3. Since the rows should be truly vertical, too, make the courses at a corner true by hanging a plumb bob (or a spike on a string) and marking the edges. Cut the tile the right size to form a vertical but fit tightly into the corner.

4. If, however, there is a prominent window, a row of complete tiles should run across the bottom. In this case make that row the starting point, and lay tiles both down and up from it.

mastic cans you'll find a diagram of the proper size and spacing for the spreader teeth. If they are too big—or too small—you may spread too much or too little mastic for the best job.

Most mastics give you about an hour of "open time" during which you can lay tile in place, gradually spreading the adhesive ahead of yourself as you go, and adjusting each piece. When you work on a floor, don't "tile" yourself into a corner. Be sure not to walk on the new tile until the mastic has set the required length of time.

On walls, you must provide support for the tiles to keep them from sliding down the wall in the fresh mastic. This is taken care of automatically with some tiles, which have tiny ridges on adjacent sides, to hold them the proper distance apart. With other tile, you may have to improvise, as covered below.

Laying the tile. This is the easy part. Tiles should be firmed into position, but without too much pressure. Be careful not to skid them, or you may squeegee the mastic up at the edge. With individual tiles, it is best to place each tile on the edge of the previous one, then gently slide it off so that it slips into position without any skidding at all.

Blocks of tiles, unitized with paper, are flexible, much the same as a piece of plastic floor tile. It is simple to hold the far edge or corner away from the adhesive while you position the critical edges, then lower the free corner into place. Smooth and press the units with the palms of your hands and spread fingers.

5. Before you start to lay tile, be sure the base is ready. Sand high spots down, checking most carefully at the floor line, where plasterers may not do a finished job.

6. It is good practice to calk around pipes that emerge from walls, if there is space. This prevents the movement of moisture through the wall.

7. Pipes have flanges (against the wall on the two supply pipes, hanging down on the waste line) that cover the broken edges of tile. You'll find it easy to nibble tile with pliers, after you scribe the curve with a glass cutter. When the hole must come in the middle of a tile, cut it in two, then nibble the space out of the two pieces equally.

8. Final step is applying grout, a thin mixture of special cement and water. Rub it into the cracks with rubber-gloved hands, then use a window squeegee to remove most of the grout on the surface. Since it doesn't adhere to the glazed surface, you can wipe away the rest after it dries.

Grouting the tile. Tile, whether unitized or laid individually, should have about $\frac{1}{16}''$ spaces, which are filled with a plastic or cementitious material that makes them watertight. Do not leave less than this amount of space. Do not leave much more. If you do you will get a poor grouting job. It is sometimes thought that you can increase or decrease the space between tiles as a means of making things come out right at the corners. This is not so. Accommodation for dimensions of the tiles vs. the dimensions of the wall must be made by cutting tiles at the corner to make proper fit. (See below.)

Standard grout comes in the form of a powder which you mix with water or in a premixed paste. There are grouts based on epoxy resins, as well as vinyl, which have the advantage of extra flexibility and elasticity, minimizing cracking between tiles. The methods for applying these materials vary from brand to brand; read the labels carefully.

To apply standard grout, you smear the paste over the surface of the tile, working it into the cracks. The object is to fill the spaces entirely. Any voids guarantee trouble later. After the grout is rubbed in thoroughly, an ordinary window squeegee is handy to clean off the majority of the remaining mastic on the surface. Then you "strike" the joints using some smooth, rounded end such as the handle of a toothbrush, leaving the grout slightly coved. While doing this operation, observe carefully the continuity of the grout, and fill in any voids that show up.

After the grout has hardened, the final step is to wipe it off the surface of the tiles, leaving them clean and smooth. An old turkish towel works well for this operation.

REMOVING BROKEN OR LOOSE TILES

You'll find it possible most of the time to salvage tiles that are loose. Use a chisel or screwdriver to pry them free. Then scrape or carefully chip away any mortar that may be clinging to the back of the tile. If necessary, use a weak solution of muriatic acid in water to remove the plaster, so that the tiles are clean. Meanwhile, remove any grout sticking to the edges.

FLOOR TILE OFTEN COME
IN UNITIZED SHEETS

Small tiles—square or in other shapes—usually come in sheets, held in proper spacing by a sheet of paper or a fine plastic net. This speeds the job of laying.

Basic step in preparation for new floor tile is reinforcement of the subfloor with an underlayment of plywood.

Underlayment gets a seal coat of waterproofing primer. Then, the mastic used for laying the tile is waterproof, too. Final step is grouting, as with wall tile.

Typical of decorative tiles dealers handle are these sealife patterns. Although they are intended for sparking up a bath when it is first tiled, they can be used for repair work when matching tiles are impossible to find. The result is a sound tiled wall once more — plus the interest and color of the patterned replacements.

If a tile is broken you can go one of these routes.

• Use Duco cement to reassemble the parts.

• Take a scrap to the tile shop and ask the man to help you match it.

• Go deliberately after mismatch. You can buy units of tiles (see photo) that form picture-like decorations. If one of these would be appropriate, chip out the number of tiles necessary and install the decorative tiles. (On a relatively small wall, you could remove a hit-and-miss, Mondrian-like pattern of tiles and replace them with accent colors, making the whole misfortune seem deliberate.)

• Or, you can get hold of a tile that matches closely. From an inconspicuous spot (back of a door, down in a corner) carefully remove a tile. Use this tile for the conspicuous patch, and use the slightly mismatching piece in the inconspicuous place.

The next job is to restore the place where the broken tile came from. It must be the same level as it was originally, which means you have to spackle-fill some low spots with patching plaster. Using this plaster, adjust the depth of the hole so that the replaced tile is flush with its neighbors. When the patching plaster has set, apply mastic to the tile, put it in place, and grout when the time comes.

Replacing a larger area. When damage (usually water) causes a fairly large area of tile to come loose, it is usually simplest to restore the wall by using a piece of asbestos board cut to fit the opening. When you utilize this method, adjust the board for depth by troweling patching cement on the existing wall, if necessary. Fasten the asbestos board in place with nails into the wall studs, unless the space involved is so small that it doesn't span two studs. When this is the case, smooth the area with patching plaster at the right depth. Apply the asbestos board with mastic. Mastic the tile in position, then grout.

THREE STEPS IN REPAIRING
SERIOUS WALL DAMAGE

1. Leaks through plaster caused wall behind tile to deteriorate completely. For repair, the first step is fitting a piece of asbestos board into the damaged area. Then apply mastic.

2. Notched trowel spreads the mastic properly. Use of waterproof adhesive guards against repeat damage.

3. Position tiles and firm them into the mastic. Normally you can use the same tiles for repairs in damage of this sort, after they have been cleaned (see text).

HANDLING WALL-SIZE TILE WORK

When repairs or replacement, or new installation, of tile involves an entire wall, you must plan the layout of the units on the area. It would be convenient if you could start at one corner of a tiling job, working across and down or across and up, willy-nilly. You can't. There are certain features of a bathroom or kitchen or other floor or wall or countertop that dictate spacing, for example, soap trays, medicine cabinets, sinks, lavatories, tissue holder, etc., not to mention the height of a bathtub.

Nor do you want to end up in a corner or at an edge with a narrow row of tiles, while another corner has tiles full width. To avoid this, find the middle of the tile run. Using a tile as a gauge, mark tile widths across the span. If, at the end, the leftover is *less than half a tile*, you should lay the wall with a full tile centered at the middle. If the leftover is *more than half a tile*, a joint belongs at the middle.

This procedure works both laterally and vertically, whether you are working with unitized mosaics, standard wall tiles, or large pavers, on horizontal or vertical surfaces. The object is, insofar as possible, to "center" the tile job on its area, surrounding it with a "frame" that is as uniform as possible.

HANDLING THE PROBLEM OF
WALL-MOUNTED FIXTURES

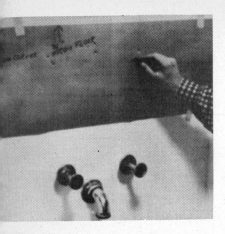
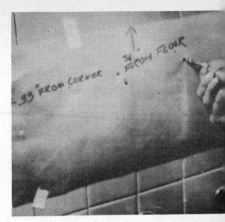

You may want to dismount such items as wall-hung lavatories. If you do, tape up a piece of paper over the area where the mounting bracket was (*left*). Probe with a pencil until you find the screw holes. Mark the position of the paper, as shown here at 33" from the corner and 36" from the floor. That way you can reposition it after the tile is in place and use a carbide-tipped bit to drill holes for remounting the bracket (*right*).

To mount a recessed soap dish or similar fixture, leave four tiles (more if the fixture is bigger) out when you lay up the wall. Cut through the plaster in back, to allow the dish to recess.

Lay the dish face down on four tiles and pencil mark its shape and size in their exact center. Score along those lines carefully with the glass cutter. Try not to run the cutter beyond the corners. Then cut a crisscross of scoring in the area to be removed.

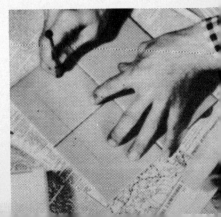

Use pliers (or nippers made especially for this kind of work) to chip out the space required for the fixture.

Coat the sides of the fixture with mastic and slip it into position. Clean away excess adhesive. When it has set, use grout to fill in neatly around the installation.

Working around a tub. The bathtub presents a special problem, since it is sound engineering to run a row of whole tiles at the top of the tub. In fact, standard built-in tubs have a lip which runs upwards at plaster level, so that tile can overlap it, making a watertight joint.

All of this dictates the height of one row of tile: the same height as the tub. From this row, you must lay tile down to the floor and up to wainscot height. (It is because the break at the ceiling may be awkward that a high wainscot is used, even in a tub-shower situation, with enamel on the wall for a short distance up to the ceiling above the tile.)

The simplest way to handle this problem is to nail to the wall a length of 1 x 2 exactly even with the top edge of the tub, and level. Lay the tile above this board. When the mastic has set beyond the sag point, remove the board. Prepare a series of vertical rows, adjusting them to exact height beneath the upper wall by cutting the tile which hits the floor, or the cove, if you are using one. Put these tiles in place in vertical rows, not horizontal, and keep the spaces proper (1/16") by lifting each tile up beneath the preceding one. Cut tiles to fit for the bottom row. Thus, if there is any discrepancy—such as lack of parallelism—it will occur at the floor, where it is least conspicuous.

In a shower stall. Water plus steam makes the job tougher for tile in a shower stall, but hardly tougher for you. The best thing to do is to line the stall with asbestos board. Then, use an epoxy mastic and grout. You may find it interesting and easier to put in the ceiling diagonally, since it removes all of the problems of matching ceiling rows with wall rows.

SOME METHODS IN SHOWERS ARE DIFFERENT

Shower floor underlayment is reinforced concrete, made by placing a sheet of half-inch hardware cloth over the area, then cutting out a hole for the drain.

Then, a 2" thickness of fine-mix concrete goes down, carefully troweled smooth. A wad of old rags in the drain keeps the concrete out of it.

On top of the troweled cement, sprinkle a thin layer of "neat cement"—with no sand. When the water has worked through this cement, lay out the sheets of tile.

At the center, install the drain ring (which accepts the seive or screen). Then use glass cutter and pliers to shape final tiles to fit around the drain. Grouting comes last. Tile dealers sell special grout for shower stall use.

The walls of a shower stall go on last. If you lay the tiles (in mastic) on the ceiling diagonally, the effect is interesting, and you bypass the difficulty of having ceiling tiles line up with those on the wall. At the edges, use half-tiles cut on the diagonal.

HOW TO CUT AND SHAPE TILE

You need three tools to cut and shape tile — and they can be improvisations. Your tile dealer may loan or rent a tile cutter to you. Otherwise, buy a new glasscutter. To smooth edges you need a file or rasp; the variety called "bastard" is best. But, you can also use aluminum oxide sandpaper, about 80 grit, on a firm smooth wooden block. And, you need a pair of "nippers," a special breed of pliers with edges that come together on the front and back of a tile, producing a fairly clean break. But you can do nearly as well with an ordinary pair of pliers.

TWO STEPS IN CUTTING TILE

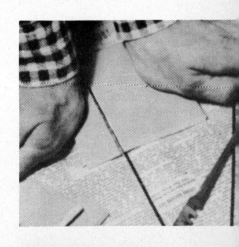

1. An ordinary glass cutter scores tile, so that you can break it by applying pressure as shown here, with the cutter mark positioned directly over a piece of wire such as a coat hanger. If you have much work to do, the tile outlet will loan or rent an efficient cutter that speeds the job.

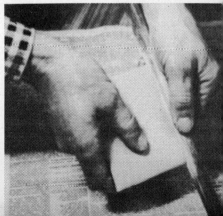

2. Make the edges of the cut smooth with a rasp of the type labeled "bastard." It is most important to have the glazed edge smooth, so the grout will show an even line.

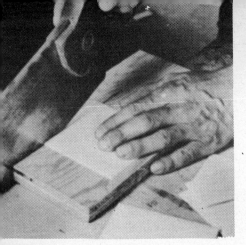

SOME TECHNIQUES ARE
DIFFERENT WITH PLASTIC TILE

Plastic tile is easy to cut with a fine-tooth saw. Shown here is a cutting board formed of a single saw-cut in a piece of plywood. Position the cutting line of the tile over this slot, and your cut will be true and smooth.

Because plastic tile is easy to cut, you'll find it easiest to leave mounting plates, etc., on the wall and fit around them, rather than removing them and remounting when tile is in place.

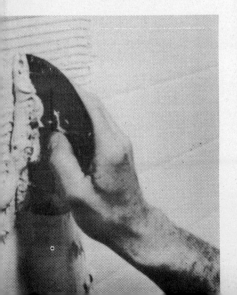

The spread of mastic back of plastic tile is a bit thicker than with clay tile, since the adhesive material is intended to ooze up between tiles, acting as a grout-like sealer.

Proper amount of mastic produces beads and strips between tiles, as shown here. Action here is placing the final cut tile in a corner.

Pencil eraser makes an excellent tool for smoothing the mastic between tiles. It gives you a neatly coved joint. When the smoothing is finished, clean away excess mastic on tile surfaces.

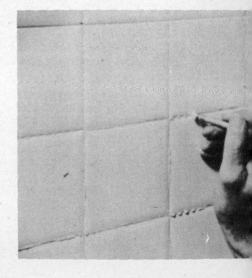

Straight cuts. Put the tile in the cutter, or lay a straightedge along it to guide the glass cutter. Score it sharply, the same as you would glass. Then position the score mark over a piece of wire (a coat hanger) and apply pressure on both sides with the heels of your hands. Click! Smooth the edges with the rasp or sandpaper.

Inside cuts. Sometimes it is necessary to cut a corner out of one or more tiles, as when you must surround a soap dish or some such. Score the lines of the shape carefully, making sure not to score beyond the point where the cut should be. Make a crisscross of score marks with the cutter over the area to be removed. Take the nippers and gradually chip out the crisscrossed unwanted area. Clean up the cut with rasp or sandpaper.

Important: Do not try to rush this job by taking bites that are too big, or you may cause the tile to break where you don't want it to.

With any cut tile, it is important mainly to have the visible edge smooth. When you grout, the joint will be neat and smooth, especially in view of the fact that the cut edge is most often in a corner or at the floor.

Spacing between tiles. Some tiles are produced with little ridges on two sides, to hold them the proper distance apart. In other cases, you have to provide the spaces, uniformly, yourself. An easy way to do this is to stock a couple of pounds of 6-penny finishing nails. Use two of them between tiles, point inward, and leave them there until the mastic sets.

REPAIR WORK ON COUNTERTOPPING

Most countertops these days are made of the rugged plastic materials called "decorative laminate," such as Formica and Micarta. They are rarely damaged, although misusing them as a cutting board will eventually destroy the surface. A hard blow with a pointed object may rupture the material by indenting the plywood it is normally mounted on. And, these materials are susceptible to scorching and burning.

Most repair work, however, is likely to involve recementing laminate which has come loose from the backing. Such adhesive failure is most likely to occur along an edge, where moisture may seep in. Although the adhesive is waterproof, the water may cause the fibers of the plywood base to loosen. When this is the case, of course, the plywood is certain to be waterlogged. Follow these steps:

• Lift the edge carefully and with a piece of wood about the size of a ruler or yardstick, continue to raise the material until you come to a corner.

• Raise the corner as far as you can without cracking the laminate, and prop it up with a stick.

• Leave it in this position until the area is entirely dry. You can speed up the drying with an electric fan, a photoflood, a hair dryer, or a little electric space heater.

• When it is dry, use coarse sandpaper to remove all the "whiskers" of wood fibers. Work as far back under the laminate as possible, but be careful not to let debris pile up in the crack, or it will result in an uneven surface.

• Use contact cement to put the material back down (see below).

Decorative laminate cuts readily with any type of hand or power saw, although saber saws tend to chip, even with a fine-tooth blade. When the cut is made, smooth the edges with an ordinary plane. A good way to hold the material steady is by clamping it between two boards, one end in the vise, as shown.

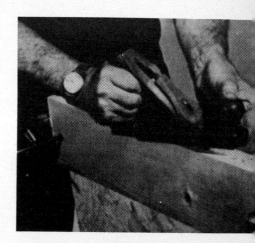

Patch a fairly large damaged area of laminate by cutting a piece of matching material big enough to cover the damage. Fasten it in place with double-faced "carpet" tape, then use it as its own pattern to cut through the laminate. Remove the cutout piece and put the new piece in place. Even with patterned laminate like this, it is usually possible to match lines in a way to make the patch inconspicuous.

When the countertopping comes loose, it is usually due to water gradually soaking the backing. Before you glue it back, raise the laminate and leave it propped up until the backing is thoroughly dry.

PATCHING IN THE MIDDLE OF AN AREA

If the damage to the plastic laminate is not at an edge, but requires a cut-out patch, the first step is to visit the dealer to see if you can pick up a piece of matching material. Cut this material to size and fasten it over the damaged area with a double-face tape, most commonly sold as "carpet tape." Adjust the patch for the best match with the pattern, if there is one.

Use a linoleum knife to scribe carefully around the patch. If you are careful, using plenty of pressure, you can cut through for a perfect fit, although it will take many passes with the knife. When the damaged material has been cut all around, use a chisel or putty knife to break it out. Clean up the exposed base. If it is dented, use an epoxy filler to make it level. Then use the contact cement process covered below to cement the patch in place.

You can never avoid a certain amount of space around the patch, and there is danger that water will find its way through, possibly causing future troubles. Guard against this by grouting some Duco cement into the cracks, filling them completely. Wipe the surplus off the surface before it dries.

USING CONTACT CEMENT

Contact cement, a material familiar to many handymen, is unlike other adhesives in use and in performance. It sticks to just about anything in its liquid form; then it sticks to itself in its dry form. In use, you brush it on both surfaces to be stuck together, let it dry, then bring the two faces together.

The bond is instant. You don't have any adjustment period. If you are lifting a corner or edge, and the position is automatic, this is of no consequence, since the sheet can't get out of line. However, when you are working with a piece of loose laminate, follow these steps:

1. Cut a piece of the laminate to exactly the size needed for the repair.

2. Brush a coat of contact cement on the back of the laminate and on the base to which it is to be applied. In some cases it may be necessary to brush on two coats; read the instructions. These coatings must dry — but not too dry. They should be dry enough so that your fingers don't stick to them, but not so dry that they feel "varnish" hard.

3. While they are drying, cut two pieces of paper, each a bit more than half the size of the area. Newspaper works, but it's better to use a heavier material such as the "tagboard" stationery stores sell, or "poster paper" you can get at art shops. Lay these two pieces of paper over the area, so that *they overlap at the center* and cover the entire space.

4. When the cement is properly dry, position the laminate carefully over the space. It will not stick to the paper, nor will the paper stick to the base.

5. Place your hand on one side of the laminate to hold it in position. With the other hand, pull the piece of paper on the other side so that there is a space of about 2″ between them.

6. Press the laminate down along this space. It will adhere to the base, and it is now locked in position.

7. Pull the pieces of paper laterally, one at a time, rubbing the laminate into contact as you remove the paper. This prevents any undesirable buckling of the material.

8. When both pieces of paper have been removed, go over the entire area, pounding it with the heel of your hand. Try

PATCHING DENTS IN
PLASTIC LAMINATE COUNTERS

1. Mix a small quantity of epoxy filler (or auto body putty) on a scrap of aluminum, and trowel it into the dent with small spatula.

2. Force the patching material into the depressions with a putty knife, at the same time squeegeeing the excess off the surface. You can wipe away the remaining filler before it sets with a rag dampened with lacquer thinner—but don't wait until it sets. A small amount of smoothing with extremely fine sandpaper will not harm the laminate.

3. Mix a tiny amount of high quality enamel with tinting colorants to match the laminate, and "stipple" it on the patches.

to hit every square inch of the laminate to force it into contact, so it will stick and stay stuck.

Use the above cementing procedures for all work with decorative laminates, where you are patching in a small area or putting a new surface on an entire counter.

PATCHING SMALL DENTS

If a plastic laminate is ruptured by a hard blow, producing a dent, you can cut it out as covered above. But, it is easier to treat the damge the way you might handle a dent in your car. Use an epoxy filler.

First, chip out the broken laminate, and the damaged base, so that the hole is sound, the way a dentist drills out a cavity before he fills it.

Mix the epoxy filler and trowel it smooth, filling the depression completely. When it has set, sand off any high spots, if necessary, but be careful not to abrade the surrounding undamaged surface.

As a final step, use a high quality enamel of the proper color to finish the patch.